The Nature of Science

You Can Do What Scientists Do . . . S2

You Can Think Like a Scientist S4

You Can Be an Inventor S10

You Can Make Decisions S14

Science Safety S16

You Can...

Do What Scientists Do

Meet Dr. Kenneth Sulak. He works for the United States Geological Survey. He studies fish and other animals that live deep in the ocean. Dr. Sulak wants to find out what kinds of animals live far below the surface. He wants to know how many of them there are and how they live. He also wants to know how deep-sea animals interact with animals in the shallower water above them.

Dr. Sulak's research depends on submersibles. A ship with a crane lowers a sub into the Gulf of Mexico. In it, Dr. Sulak can travel far below the surface to observe and collect deep-sea life.

HARBOR BRANCH
OCEANOGRAPHIC

Ocean fishing, exploring for oil, and other human activities are moving into deeper and deeper water. Dr. Sulak helps keep track of how these activities affect deep-sea life. He shares what he learns by speaking to and answering the questions of other scientists. He also writes about it in science magazines.

Scientists investigate in different ways.

The ways scientists investigate depend on the questions they ask. Dr. Sulak observes animals in their natural habitats. He also classifies animals. Often, he measures water temperatures. Other scientists ask questions that can be answered by doing a fair test called an experiment.

Dr. Kenneth Sulak uses a microscope to learn more about deep-sea life. He has been surprised to discover how many animals live very deep in the ocean and that many deep-sea animals are bright red.

Think Like a Scientist

The ways scientists ask and answer questions about the world around them is called **scientific inquiry.** Scientific inquiry requires certain attitudes, or ways of thinking. To think like a scientist you have to be:

- curious and ask a lot of questions.

- creative and think up new ways to do things.

- able to keep an open mind. That means you listen to the ideas of others.

- open to changing what you think when your investigation results surprise you.

- willing to question what other people tell you.

Tides are changes in the level of the ocean that occur each day. What causes tides?

Use Critical Thinking

When you think critically you make decisions about what others tell you or what you read. Is what you heard or read fact or opinion? A *fact* can be checked to make sure it is true. An *opinion* is what you think about the facts.

Did anyone ever tell you how something works that you found hard to believe? When you ask, "What facts back up your idea?" you are thinking critically. Critical thinkers question scientific statements.

Tides seem to rise and fall at about the same time each day. I wonder what causes tides to keep changing that way?

I read that tides are caused by the pull of the Moon's gravity on Earth's oceans. The level of the oceans keeps rising and falling as the Moon and Earth move into different positions.

Science Inquiry

Using scientific inquiry helps you understand the world around you. For example, suppose you collect a sample of water from the ocean and put it in the freezer over night.

Observe The next day, you notice that the ocean water is not completely frozen. You also notice that ice cubes in the freezer are frozen solid.

Ask a Question When you think about what you saw, heard, or read, you may have questions.

Hypothesis Think about facts you already know. Do you have an idea about the answer? Write it down. That is your hypothesis.

Experiment Plan a test that will tell if the hypothesis is true or not. List the materials and tools you will need. Write the steps you will follow. Make sure that you keep all conditions the same except the one you are testing. That condition is called the *variable.*

Conclusion What do your results tell you? Do they support your hypothesis or show it to be false?

Describe your experiment with enough detail that others can repeat it. Communicate your results and conclusion.

My Salt Water Experiment

Observe It seems that ocean water does not freeze at the same temperature as plain water. Ocean water is salty.

Ask a question I wonder if salt lowers the freezing point of water?

Hypothesis Salt water freezes at a lower temperature than plain water.

Experiment I'll put the same amount of salt water and plain water in a freezer. I'll lower the temperature in the freezer until both kinds of water turn to ice. I'll record the temperatures at which the plain water and salt water freeze.

Conclusion Salt water turns to ice at a lower temperature than plain water. The results support my hypothesis. Salt water has a lower freezing point than plain water.

Inquiry Process

Here is a process that some scientists follow to answer questions and make new discoveries.

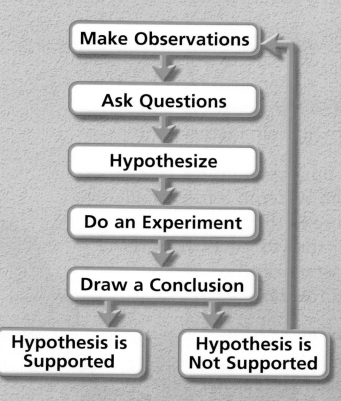

Make Observations

↓

Ask Questions

↓

Hypothesize

↓

Do an Experiment

↓

Draw a Conclusion

↓

Hypothesis is Supported

Hypothesis is Not Supported

Science Inquiry Skills

You'll use many of these inquiry skills when you investigate and experiment.

- Ask Questions
- Observe
- Compare
- Classify
- Predict
- Measure

- Hypothesize
- Use Variables
- Experiment
- Use Models
- Communicate
- Use Numbers

- Record Data
- Analyze Data
- Infer
- Collaborate
- Research

Try It Yourself!

Experiment With an Energy Sphere

When you touch both metal strips of the Energy Sphere, the sphere lights. This works with two people—as long as they are in contact with one another.

1 What questions do you have about the Energy Sphere?

2 How would you find out the answers?

3 Write your experiment plan and predict what will happen.

You Can...

Be an Inventor

Alberto Behar's interest in space led him to a career in space engineering. Dr. Behar helped to invent a new kind of Martian rover. Called the tumbleweed, it looks more like a giant beach ball than a vehicle. It moves when the wind blows it.

The idea for the tumbleweed came about by accident. During a test of a rover with large inflatable wheels, one of the wheels fell off. The wind blew the wheel several kilometers before someone caught it. The idea of a wind-blown rover was born.

The tumbleweed has performed very well in tests on Earth. Dr. Behar thinks it may soon be used to explore the surface of Mars.

"When I was about seven or eight, I wanted to be an astronaut. I checked out all of the books on space I could at the library..."

What Is Technology?

The tools people make and the things they build with tools are all technology. A toy car is technology. So is a race car.

Scientists use technology, too. For example, a laser beam can be used to make very precise measurements. Scientists also use microscopes to see things they cannot see with just their eyes.

Many technologies make the world a better place to live. But sometimes a technology that solves one problem can cause other problems. For example, farmers use fertilizer to increase the yields of their crops. But fertilizer can be carried by rain water into lakes and streams where it can harm fish and other living things.

A Better Idea

"I wish I had a better way to _____." How would you fill in the blank? Everyone wishes they could find a way to do their jobs more easily or have more fun. Inventors try to make those wishes come true. Inventing or improving an invention requires time and patience.

George Hansburg patented the pogo stick in 1919. It was a Y-shaped metal stick with two foot rests and a spring. Today's pogo sticks are not much different.

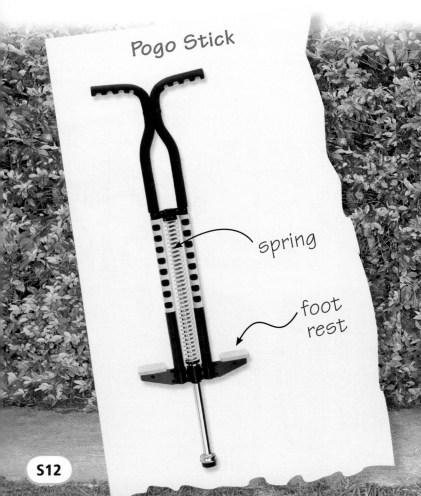

Pogo Stick

spring

foot rest

How to Be an Inventor

1. **Identify a problem.** It may be a problem at school, at home, or in your community.

2. **List ways to solve the problem.** Sometimes the solution is a new tool. Other times it may be a new way of doing an old job or activity.

3. **Choose the best solution.** Decide which idea you predict will work best. Think about which one you can carry out.

4. **Make a sample.** A sample, called a *prototype,* is the first try. Your idea may need many materials or none at all. Choose measuring tools that will help your design work better.

5. **Try out your invention.** Use your prototype, or ask someone else to try it. Keep a record of how it works and what problems you find. The more times you try it, the more information you will have.

6. **Improve your invention.** Use what you learned to make your design work better. Draw or write about the changes you make and why you made them.

7. **Share your invention.** Show your invention to others. Explain how it works. Tell how it makes an activity easier or more fun. If it did not work as well as you wanted, tell why.

Make Decisions

Trouble for the Everglades

For many years, the water of the Florida Everglades has had too much phosphorus. The phosphorus comes from nearby farms and cities. Phosphorus in fertilizers washes into streams and rivers. Phosphorus in laundry detergents washes down drains. Much of the phosphorus ends up in the water of the Everglades.

Some types of plants and animals have not been able to stand the high phosphorus levels. They have decreased in numbers or even gone extinct. Scientists are trying to reduce the amount of phosphorus entering the Everglades. They are also looking for ways to remove the phosphorus that is already there.

Deciding What to Do

What methods are best to help lower phosphorus levels in the water of the Everglades?

Here's how to make your decision about the phosphorus problem. You can use the same steps to help solve problems in your home, in your school, and in your community.

 **Learn** → Learn about the problem. Take the time needed to get the facts. You could talk to an expert, read a science book, or explore a web site.

List → Make a list of actions you could take. Add actions other people could take.

Decide → Think about each action on your list. Decide which choice is the best one for you or your community.

 **Share** → Communicate your decision to others.

Phosphorus In The Everglades

Sources of Phosphorus
- Fertilizers
- Detergents
- Other Sources

Phosphorus Level

Solutions

Year

Science Safety

☑ Know the safety rules of your school and classroom and follow them.

☑ Read and follow the safety tips in each Investigation activity.

☑ When you plan your own investigations, write down how to keep safe.

☑ Know how to clean up and put away science materials. Keep your work area clean and tell your teacher about spills right away.

☑ Know how to safely plug in electrical devices.

☑ Wear safety goggles when your teacher tells you.

☑ Unless you teacher tells you to, never put any science materials in or near your ears, eyes, or mouth.

☑ Wear gloves when handling live animals.

☑ Wash your hands when your investigation is done.

Caring for Living Things

☑ Learn how to care for the plants and animals in your classroom so that they stay healthy and safe. Learn how to hold animals carefully.

The Nature of Matter

The Nature of Matter

Chapter 12
Properties of Matter.....................................E2

Chapter 13
How Matter Changes..............................E34

Independent Reading

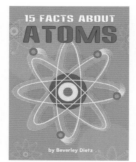

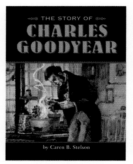

I Can Measure an Elephant

15 Facts About Atoms

The Story of Charles Goodyear

A hot-air balloon weighs more than 4,000 pounds and is as tall as a seven-story building. Yet the balloon rises and floats across the sky. How does a hot-air balloon rise and stay in the air? You will have the answer to this question by the end of this unit.

Chapter **12**

Properties of Matter

LESSON

1 Solid ice, rushing water, and invisible water vapor—how does water take such different forms?

Read about it in Lesson 1.

LESSON

2 Your weight on the Moon and your weight on Earth—how would it vary?

Read about it in Lesson 2.

LESSON

3 The bright color of a flower or the rough texture of a tree trunk—what are some other ways to describe matter?

Read about it in Lesson 3.

What Makes Up Matter?

Why It Matters...

Matter is everywhere. The air you breathe, the water you drink, and the clothes you wear are made of it. You can see matter as an interesting sculpture or smell it as the odor of a flower. You can even taste it as a delicious meal. Matter is made up of very small pieces too small to see.

PREPARE TO INVESTIGATE

Inquiry Skill

Observe When you observe, you gather information about the environment using your five senses: seeing, hearing, smelling, touching, and tasting.

Materials

- sugar cube
- granulated sugar
- powdered sugar
- plastic spoon
- black construction paper
- hand lens

Science and Math Toolbox

For step 4, review **Using a Hand Lens** on page H2.

Compare Matter

Procedure

1. **Collaborate** Work with a partner. In your *Science Notebook*, make a chart like the one shown.

2. Place a sugar cube, a spoonful of granulated sugar, and a spoonful of powdered sugar on a sheet of black paper. Label each sugar sample. **Safety:** Do not taste the sugar samples.

3. **Observe** Look at the color and texture of each sugar sample. Break off a small piece of the sugar cube and rub it between your fingers. Now rub a small amount of each of the other two samples between your fingers. Note how hard or soft each sample feels. Record your observations in your chart.

4. **Observe** Use a hand lens to observe each sugar sample. Record your observations.

Conclusion

1. **Compare** What differences did you observe when you looked at the sugar samples without a hand lens? With a hand lens? How were the samples alike?

2. **Infer** Which do you think contains more small pieces, or particles, of sugar—the spoonful of granulated sugar or the spoonful of powdered sugar? Explain.

STEP 1

Method of Observation	Sugar Cube	Granulated Sugar	Powdered Sugar
Eyes			
Hand Lens			

STEP 2

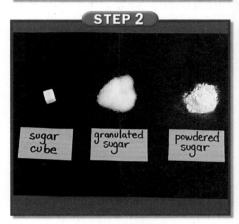

STEP 4

Investigate More!

Design an Experiment Tiny solid particles float in the air outdoors. Using clear sticky tape, plan an experiment to collect these particles. Then use a microscope or hand lens to look at them.

Matter Everywhere

VOCABULARY

atom   p. E7
matter   p. E6
molecule   p. E7
physical property p. E10
states of matter p. E8

READING SKILL

Main Idea and Details
Use a chart to show the main idea and two details of the lesson.

MAIN IDEA Matter is anything that has mass and takes up space. It may be a solid, a liquid, or a gas.

Observing Matter

Look around you. What do you see? Perhaps you see desks and other people. Is there anything you can feel, but not see? You may feel a breeze blowing across your face.

These are examples of matter. **Matter** is anything that has mass and takes up space. Everything that you can see is matter. Even things you cannot see, such as air, are matter.

Matter has many different properties. Color, size, shape, and texture are just a few of these properties. Some properties can be observed only by using a microscope or a hand lens.

A Closer Look

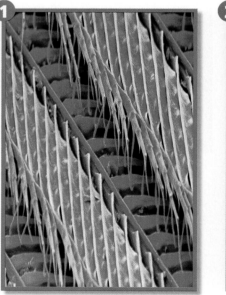

Scientists use microscopes to magnify objects to observe the properties of matter. Look at the magnified objects. What do you think each one is? (The answers are at the bottom of the next page.)

Notice how different an object looks when it is magnified. By studying matter with very powerful microscopes, scientists have learned that all matter is made up of very tiny particles. These particles are always moving.

The smallest particle of matter that has the properties of that matter is called an **atom** (AT uhm). All objects contain a very large number of atoms. There are more atoms in one grain of sand than there are people on Earth!

Most matter is made up of atoms that have combined with other atoms to make a molecule (MAHL ih kyool). A **molecule** is a single particle of matter that is made up of two or more atoms joined together. The smallest particle of water is a molecule made up of three atoms.

Scientists have learned from studying atoms and molecules that two objects cannot take up the same space at the same time. If you put your book on the desk, can you put your pencils in the exact same place? Of course not! When one object takes up space, nothing else can take up that space at that exact moment. This is true for all matter, even air!

▶ **MAIN IDEA** **What is the smallest particle of matter?**

1. feather; 2. fly's eye; 3. salt; 4. nylon fibers; 5. shampoo; 6. dentist's drill

Three States of Matter

Whoosh! Look at that geyser! A rush of steam bursts into the air on a winter day. You can see three different forms, or states, of water in this scene—or can you? The **states of matter** are three forms that matter usually takes: solid, liquid, and gas. The ice on the ground is a solid. The water in the pool and the mist above it are liquids. You cannot see water as a gas. Water vapor is invisible.

The three states of water—ice, water, and water vapor—look very different. These different states have very different properties. However, ice, water, and water vapor are alike in one important way—they are all the same kind of matter. Each particle of ice, water, and water vapor is made up of the same kind of molecule. Each of these molecules is made up of the same combination of three atoms.

What causes solids, liquids, and gases to have different properties? The particles of matter in different states are arranged differently. Look at the diagrams to find out how.

▶ **MAIN IDEA** How are ice, water, and water vapor alike?

Water
Water is a liquid. The molecules in a liquid slide past each other but stay close together. They do not form a regular pattern.

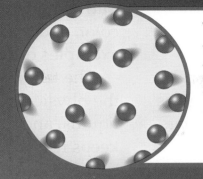

Water Vapor

Water vapor is a gas. The molecules of a gas are not arranged in any pattern. They move rapidly and do not stay close together.

Ice

Ice is a solid. The molecules of a solid are packed together in a regular pattern. They vibrate back and forth in place.

Properties of Solids, Liquids, and Gases

How can you tell that water is inside this tea kettle? The steam gives a clue. Matter changes from one state to another without becoming a new kind of matter. The state of matter is an example of a physical property (FIHZ ih kuhl PRAHP ur tee) of matter. A **physical property** is a characteristic of matter that can be observed without changing matter into something new. Size, shape, color, and texture are other examples of physical properties.

The table below compares the physical properties of solids, liquids, and gases. A solid always keeps its shape. A liquid takes the shape of its container. A gas spreads apart or can be squeezed together to fit into a given space.

▶ **MAIN IDEA** What is a physical property?

States of Matter

State of Matter	Shape	Size
Solid	Definite shape	Fixed size
Liquid	No definite shape	Fixed size
Gas	No definite shape	No fixed size

The clear space above the spout is water vapor, a gas. The cloud above the space is not a gas. It is water droplets mixed in air.

Visual Summary

All matter has mass and takes up space. Matter is made up of atoms and molecules.

The three states of matter are solid, liquid, and gas. Solids and liquids have a definite size. Gases do not.

Some physical properties of matter are its state, size, shape, color, and texture.

LINKS for Home and School

SOCIAL STUDIES **Research Democritus** Ancient Greek philosophers came up with the idea of atoms long before scientists were able to see them. Use the library or Internet to find out who Democritus was and what he believed about particles of matter. Share what you learn with your classmates.

ART **Make Microscope Art** The newest scanning electron microscopes can see things as small as an atom. Many materials look patterned when greatly magnified. Collect or copy images of objects at high magnifications and make a microscope collage.

Review

❶ **MAIN IDEA** Explain why the color blue and the number 12 are not considered matter.

❷ **VOCABULARY** What is the difference between an atom and a molecule?

❸ **READING SKILL: Main Idea and Details** List two details that support the idea that matter has properties that can be observed.

❹ **CRITICAL THINKING: Apply** Explain why people use solids and not liquids or gases to build houses.

❺ **INQUIRY SKILL: Observe** Choose one of the six magnified objects on pages E6 and E7. What properties of the object do you observe?

✓ **TEST PREP**
The particles of a gas ___.

A. are arranged in a pattern.

B. are spread far apart.

C. are very close together.

D. never move.

Technology
Visit **www.eduplace.com/scp/** to investigate more about states of matter.

How Is Matter Measured?

Why It Matters...

Suppose you are measuring this hamster. Using a balance is just one way to measure. How else could you measure the hamster? What tools could you use? You can measure objects to learn more about the world around you.

PREPARE TO INVESTIGATE

Inquiry Skill

Measure When you measure, you use tools to find the length or mass of an object.

Materials

- balance
- metric ruler
- 5 small classroom objects (pencil, paper clip, chalk, eraser, coin)

Science and Math Toolbox

For step 2, review **Using a Balance** on page H9.

Measure It

Procedure

1 **Collaborate** Work with a partner. In your *Science Notebook*, make a chart like the one shown. Select five small objects from around the classroom. For example, you might choose a pencil, a paper clip, a piece of chalk, an eraser, and a coin.

2 **Measure** Use a balance to find the mass of each object. Record your measurements in your chart. Be sure to use the correct units of measure for mass.

3 **Measure** Use a metric ruler to find the length of each object. Record your measurements in the chart. Be sure to use the correct units of measure for length.

Conclusion

1. **Communicate** Make a bar graph to show the mass of each object you measured. Make a second bar graph to show the lengths of the objects.

2. **Analyze Data** Which object has the greatest mass? Which has the least?

3. **Analyze Data** Which object is the longest? Which is the shortest?

STEP 1

Object	Mass	Length

STEP 2

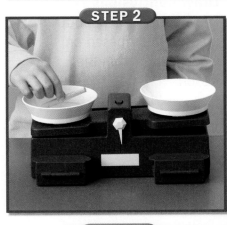

STEP 3

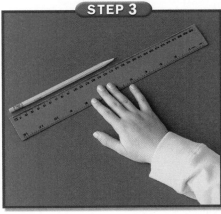

Investigate More!

Design an Experiment
Find five more objects. Predict how their masses and lengths will compare to the objects you have already measured. Check your predictions by measuring the objects.

Measuring Matter

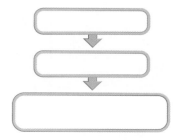

MAIN IDEA Scientists use the metric system to measure objects. Objects can be measured to find their mass and volume.

The Metric System

How could you find the exact height of a giraffe? By measuring it, of course! People have been measuring objects to describe their properties exactly for hundreds of years. At first, people used their hands or feet as measuring tools. But the measurements differed from one person to another.

Over time, scientists developed a standard system of measurement. Now scientists can easily communicate their observations about matter to other scientists. All scientists use the metric system (MEHT rihk SIHS tuhm). The **metric system** is a system of measurement based on multiples of 10. The table shows how different metric units are related.

Metric Units Conversion Chart

Property Measured	Metric Unit	Converts To
Length	1 centimeter (cm)	10 millimeters (mm)
	1 meter (m)	100 centimeters (cm)
	1 kilometer (km)	1,000 meters (m)
Volume	1 liter (L)	1,000 milliliters (mL)
Mass	1 kilogram (kg)	1,000 grams (g)

Metric Ruler (cm) ▼

0 1 2 3 4 5 6 7 8 9 10 11 12 13 14 15 16 17 18 19

Find centimeter, meter, and kilometer in the table. These units are metric units of length. You can see that 100 centimeters is the same as 1 meter. Both 1 and 100 are multiples of 10. You can easily convert between units simply by multiplying or dividing by a multiple of 10. This is true for all metric units.

When scientists measure objects, they use tools that measure in metric units. The ruler below measures length in centimeters. The giraffe's height is measured in meters.

To find out how much mass something has, scientists use a balance that measures grams or kilograms. Scientists use beakers or graduated cylinders marked in liters or milliliters to measure the volume of liquids.

▶ **DRAW CONCLUSIONS** **What metric units could be used to measure an amount of juice?**

Giraffes are one of the tallest animals in the world. Many grow to more than 5.5 m tall.

The mass of a bowling ball can be over 7 kg.

0   21   22   23   24   25   26   27   28   29   30

Mass

Suppose you hold two blocks, one in each hand. They are the same size, color, shape, and texture. However, one block feels heavier than the other. To describe exactly the difference between these blocks, you can measure their masses. **Mass** is the amount of matter in an object. The block that feels heavier has more mass—and more matter.

Mass is an important physical property used to identify, sort, and describe objects. All matter, even air and tiny particles that cannot be seen, have mass. Scientists use a balance to measure mass exactly.

To measure the mass of a block, you place it on one pan of the balance. Then you add objects with known masses, such as 1-gram or 1-kilogram standards, to the other pan. When the pans balance, the total mass of the standards equals the mass of the block.

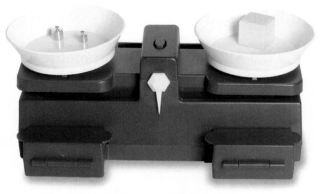

The standards on the left side of the balance have the same total mass as the block on the right side.

Volume

Another physical property of matter that is measured exactly is volume (VAHL yoom). **Volume** is the amount of space that matter takes up. As with mass, all matter has volume, even air and very tiny particles.

Volume is measured in different ways depending on the object. The volume of a liquid is measured directly with a beaker or graduated cylinder. Liters and milliliters are the metric units of volume.

To find the volume of a rectangular solid, such as this block, multiply together its length, width, and height. Its volume can be described in cubic centimeters. One cubic centimeter has the same volume as one milliliter.

How can you measure the volume of a rock? Carefully place the rock into a graduated cylinder partly filled with water and measure the change in water volume.

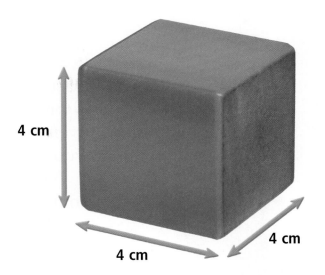

4 cm

4 cm

4 cm

The volume of a rectangular solid is equal to length times width, times height. This cube has a volume of 12 cubic centimeters (12 cm³).

▶ **DRAW CONCLUSIONS** **How can you find the volume of a block?**

The change in water volume is the volume of the rock.

▲ The spring scale measures the weight of the bear cub. Weight is a measure of the pull of gravity on an object.

Weight

How much does this bear weigh? Is its weight (wayt) the same as its mass? No. Remember that mass is the amount of matter in an object. **Weight** is the measure of the pull of gravity on an object. Even if this bear went to the Moon, its mass would stay the same.

A bear's weight, however, changes depending on the amount of gravity pulling on it. Its weight is slightly different on top of Mount Everest from its weight at sea level. If this bear went to the Moon, it would weigh even less. Why? The difference in weight is actually the difference in the amount of gravity pulling on the bear. On top of the mountain, the bear is farther away from the center of Earth, so the pull of gravity is slightly less. The pull of gravity on the Moon is very weak, so objects weigh much less on the Moon than they do on Earth.

▶ **MAIN IDEA**   **What is weight?**

Weight and Mass

Gravity gets weaker farther away from the center of Earth. At the top of a mountain, the bear weighs slightly less than 140 pounds. The bear's mass, however, is still the same.

Mountain Top

At sea level, the bear weighs 140 pounds.

Sea Level

Lesson Wrap-Up

Visual Summary

Scientists use the appropriate units of the metric system to measure the properties of matter.

Mass is the amount of matter in an object. Volume is the amount of space an object takes up.

Weight is the pull of Earth's gravity on an object. Weight varies; mass stays the same.

for Home and School

MATH **Convert in Metrics** What is the mass of the following objects in grams: a bowling ball—7 kg; a book—0.85 kg.

WRITING **Explanatory** Have you ever opened a box of cereal and wondered why it looked only half full? Food manufacturers often put a note like this on cereal boxes and packages of other foods: *Product sold by weight, not by volume.* Write an explanation of why some foods are measured by weight and not by volume.

Review

① **MAIN IDEA** What units would a scientist most likely use to measure the length of a small object?

② **VOCABULARY** Write a paragraph about measuring matter. Use the terms *mass* and *volume* in the paragraph.

③ **READING SKILL: Draw Conclusions** An object has a mass of 42 g on Earth. What is its mass on the Moon?

④ **CRITICAL THINKING: Evaluate** What would you say to someone who said that the metric system is not important?

⑤ **INQUIRY SKILL: Measure** Use the metric ruler shown on pages E14 and E15. How many centimeters long is your pen or pencil?

✓ **TEST PREP**
A backyard is 1,800 cm wide. How many meters wide is it?

A. 18,000 m

B. 1,800 m

C. 180 m

D. 18 m

Technology
Visit **www.eduplace.com/scp/** to learn more about measuring matter.

Gertrude Elion
(1918-1999)

Who invents medicines that save lives? Gertrude Belle Elion helped invent over 40 medicines that have saved thousands of lives.

When Gertrude "Trudy" Elion was 15 years old, she knew she wanted to become a scientist. She was determined to find a treatment for cancer after her beloved grandfather died of the disease. But in the 1930s, women didn't work in research laboratories. Even with a chemistry degree, Trudy struggled to find a job.

In the 1940s, many men left the United States to fight in World War II. This opened up jobs for women. In 1944, a medical company hired Trudy. She worked with Dr. George Hitchings to find a medicine to treat cancer. By 1949, they had created a chemical compound that slowed the growth of cancer cells. Trudy spent years improving the drug known as 6-MP, which still helps cancer patients today.

Trudy Elion and George Hitchings
Trudy once compared her work researching new medicines to trying to solve a mystery story.

Elion receives the Nobel Prize
Trudy won a Nobel Prize in 1988 for the invention of 6-MP. This drug is used to treat leukemia. She shared this award with Dr. George Hitchings. In 1991, she became the first woman in the National Inventors Hall of Fame.

Elion in her laboratory
When Trudy started working at the medical company, there was only one other woman on a staff of 75.

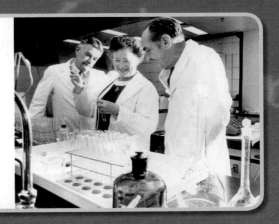

This patent names Gertrude Elion and George Hitchings as inventors of 6-MP.

Sharing Ideas

1. **READING CHECK** For what important discovery did Gertrude Belle Elion win the Nobel Prize?

2. **WRITE ABOUT IT** How do you think Trudy felt when she was hired by the medical company? Write an entry about this event in a diary that Trudy might have kept.

3. **TALK ABOUT IT** Discuss the challenges Dr. Elion faced because she was a woman.

What Are Physical and Chemical Properties?

Why It Matters...

Why are winter hats made from yarn? Perhaps it's because yarn is soft, fuzzy, and flexible. Hats would be scratchy if they were made from paper. They wouldn't hold up well in a blizzard either. A hat made from metal wouldn't fit snugly on your head. It also wouldn't keep you very warm.

PREPARE TO INVESTIGATE

Inquiry Skill

Predict When you predict, you state what you think will happen based on observations and experiences.

Materials

- 2 small, clear plastic cups
- unknown liquid A
- unknown liquid B
- masking tape
- graduated cylinder
- goggles

Science and Math Toolbox

For step 5, review **Measuring Volume** on page H7.

Compare Liquids

Procedure

1. **Collaborate** Work with a partner. In your *Science Notebook*, make a chart like the one shown.

2. **Observe** Pour equal amounts of each liquid into separate clear plastic cups. Label the containers *Liquid A* and *Liquid B*. Observe how each liquid looks. Record your observations in your chart. **Safety:** Wear goggles when pouring liquids.

3. **Compare** Carefully lift each cup. Which one seems heavier? Record your observations in your chart.

4. **Predict** What do you think will happen when you pour the two liquids into the same container? Record your prediction.

5. **Experiment** Pour 10 mL of each liquid into a graduated cylinder. What happens? Record your observations.

Conclusion

1. **Analyze Data** How does your prediction compare with the results of your experiment?

2. **Infer** What can you infer about the mass of the two liquids based on your observations?

3. **Hypothesize** Why is it important to use an equal amount of each liquid to compare their masses?

STEP 1

Unknown Liquid	How It Looks	How Heavy It Seems
Liquid A		
Liquid B		

STEP 2

STEP 5

Investigate More!

Design an Experiment
Think about how you can compare the masses of milk and fruit juice. Would you use the same method as you used in this investigation? Would you try something different?

VOCABULARY

chemical property	p. E27
density	p. E25

READING SKILL

Compare and Contrast
Use the chart to compare and contrast physical properties and chemical properties.

Physical and Chemical Properties

MAIN IDEA Matter has different physical and chemical properties. Physical and chemical properties are used to describe and classify matter.

Physical Properties

In the morning you walk to school with your blue backpack. At lunch you eat a large sandwich. At night you sleep in your soft bed. The words "blue," "large," and "soft" all describe physical properties of matter. Any sample of matter can be described by its physical properties.

Color One way to describe matter is by color. For example, flowers may be yellow or red or yellow and red. Objects may be a single color or several colors.

Shape Another way to describe matter is by shape. An object may have an easily recognizable shape, such as a sphere or a pyramid. Many objects do not have a regular shape. How would you describe the shape of your hand?

Some Physical Properties

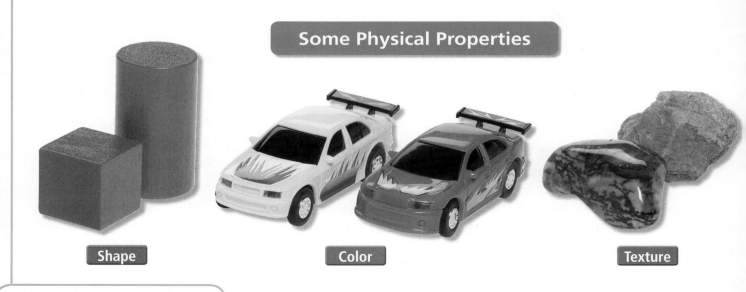

Shape   Color   Texture

Each solid object sinks through a liquid less dense than itself and floats on a liquid more dense than itself. How does the density of the grape compare to the densities of the three liquids?

Oil The liquid with the lowest density is on top.

Water The liquid with neither the lowest density nor the highest density is in the middle.

Corn syrup The liquid with the highest density is at the bottom.

Texture The texture (TEHKS chur) of an object describes how the object feels. Wool has a rough texture. Glass windows are smooth. Luster describes how the surface of an object looks when light shines on it. A mirror is very shiny, but a piece of black construction paper is not.

Density Another physical property that describes matter is density (DEHN sih tee). **Density** describes how much matter is in a given space, or volume. Because one cubic centimeter of steel has more mass than one cubic centimeter of cotton, steel is denser than cotton.

If you know the mass and volume of an object, you can calculate that object's density. Density is usually described as mass per volume with the metric units grams per cubic centimeter.

The density of a substance determines whether it will float or sink in water or another liquid. If a substance is more dense than water, it will sink. If it is less dense than water, it will float.

▶ **COMPARE AND CONTRAST** What are five physical properties that can be used to compare two samples of matter?

Useful Physical Properties

Every type of matter has its own set of physical properties. These properties affect how we use each type of matter. You would not use ice to make a chair. Although ice keeps its shape at very cold temperatures, it would melt in your classroom. A chair made of wood, metal, or plastic will keep its shape at room temperature.

Look at your desk. Does it look anything like the desk in the picture? Of course not! What kind of matter is your desk made of? What physical properties of this matter make it suitable for a desk? Your desk is likely made from many different kinds of matter. The legs of your desk are made of matter that is rigid and strong, like metal or wood. The top might be made of wood or plastic. They are solid, rigid, and strong. The top is also smooth so that you can easily write or draw on it. Is the color of the matter used to make your desk important? It might be if you chose a white desk over a brown one.

Properties that make matter useful for one purpose do not always make it useful for another. Glass is perfect to use for windows but not for swim goggles. It shatters too easily.

This desk top is made from foam rubber. What will happen when the boy puts the books on it? ▼

◄ Like physical properties, the chemical properties of matter affect how matter is used. Wood can be burned as fuel. The ashes of these burnt logs cannot be used as fuel.

Both the logs and the boards that are cut from them will burn. They are both made of wood. They differ only in their physical properties. ▶

Chemical Properties

Compare the burnt log to the cut log. The logs differ in size, shape, and texture, which you have learned are physical properties. Would you be able to burn the burnt log again? Probably not. In this way, the burnt log differs from a cut log, as well as from boards that are cut from the log.

The ability to burn is a property of matter called a chemical (KEHM-ih kuhl) property. A **chemical property** is a characteristic of matter that can be observed only when matter is changed into a new kind of matter. After burning, wood becomes ash. Ash is made of a different kind of matter than wood.

If you leave an iron nail outside in the rain, it will get rusty. The ability to rust is another example of a chemical property.

▶ **COMPARE AND CONTRAST** How is a chemical property different than a physical property?

Cooking an egg causes new kinds of matter to form.

Describing Chemical Properties

Look at the egg sizzling in the frying pan. How does cooking change the properties of an egg? You couldn't use the cooked egg to make cookie dough. Heat has changed the raw egg into something different. The ability of matter to change into a new kind of matter when heated is a chemical property.

Has the frying pan changed? After heating, the frying pan is still the same kind of matter, only warmer. The frying pan has had only a physical change, not a chemical change.

Chemical properties are often related to how matter reacts with air, heat, and water. Cooking describes how some kinds of matter undergo a chemical change when heated. Other chemical properties include the ability to burn, rust, explode, and tarnish. You can observe these properties only when you try to change matter. An iron nail will rust if it gets wet. However a nail will not burn. A toothpick will not rust, but it will burn easily.

You can use chemical properties to classify matter in the same way you use physical properties to classify matter. The ability to burn is a chemical property of wood, but is not a chemical property of silver. The ability to tarnish is a chemical property of silver, but is not a chemical property of wood.

▶ **MAIN IDEA** Give an example of a chemical property.

Visual Summary

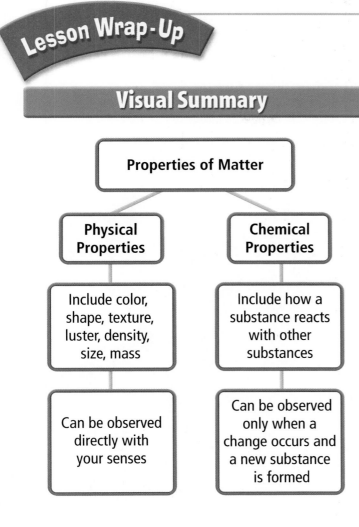

Properties of Matter

Physical Properties

Include color, shape, texture, luster, density, size, mass

Can be observed directly with your senses

Chemical Properties

Include how a substance reacts with other substances

Can be observed only when a change occurs and a new substance is formed

 **for Home and School**

TECHNOLOGY Broadcast the News
Concrete is a material that has many uses. Scientists are looking for new ways to change the density and other physical properties of concrete. Research how technology is changing concrete. Give a news broadcast to your class about what you learn.

LITERATURE Compose a Poem
Write a poem about a chemical change such as burning or rusting. Describe the physical properties of the substance before and after the chemical change.

Review

1 MAIN IDEA What are some physical and chemical properties of paper that can be observed?

2 VOCABULARY Use the term *density* in a sentence about physical properties.

3 READING SKILL: Compare and Contrast Compare and contrast the physical and chemical properties of a log and a board cut from the log.

4 CRITICAL THINKING: Synthesize When placed in water, object A floats and object B sinks. The objects are the same size and shape. Describe the masses of the objects.

5 INQUIRY SKILL: Predict Suppose you drop a solid cube into a jar containing oil and water. The cube has a higher density than the oil and a lower density than the water. Predict what will happen to the cube.

✓ TEST PREP
One chemical property is ___.

A. color.

B. density.

C. how it reacts to water.

D. how it reacts to being cut.

💻 Technology
Visit **www.eduplace.com/scp/** to find out more about chemical properties.

EXTREME Science

Vanishing Bottles

What's going on with these bottles? Why are they falling apart like that? Actually, it's a good thing they are disintegrating. They were designed to do that so that they don't become a permanent part of the mountains of trash produced every day.

These bottles are made of a kind of plastic that is biodegradable. Biodegradable means that the plastic has the chemical properties necessary to be broken down by microorganisms like bacteria and molds. Microorganisms literally eat this kind of plastic, turning it into a kind of mush or powder.

Many kinds of plastic are not biodegradable. The result is that some plastics can exist in landfills and trash dumps for hundreds, perhaps even thousands of years.

Day 1

Most plastic is not biodegradable. If a Pharaoh had drunk from a plastic bottle that wasn't biodegradable, that bottle might last as long as the stone pyramids – thousands of years!

Going, going, gone!

Day 30 **Day 50** **Day 64**

Vocabulary

Complete each sentence with a term from the list.

1. Size, shape, color, or texture is an example of a/an _____.

2. The _____ are three forms that matter usually takes: solid, liquid, and gas.

3. The _____ of an object is the amount of matter it contains.

4. A particle of matter made up of two or more atoms joined together is called a/an _____.

5. The physical property that describes how much mass is in a given space, or volume, is called _____.

6. The _____ of a sample of matter is the amount of space it takes up.

7. A/an _____ is the smallest particle of matter that has the properties of that matter.

8. A characteristic of matter that can be observed only when matter is changed into a new kind of matter is called a/an _____.

9. Meters, grams, and liters are units of the _____.

10. Anything that has mass and takes up space is _____.

atom E7
chemical property E27
density E25
mass E16
matter E6
metric system E14
molecule E7
physical property E10
states of matter E8
volume E17
weight E18

Test Prep

Write the letter of the best answer choice.

11. Weight is a measure of _____.

   A. the amount of space an object takes up.
   B. how fast the particles in an object move.
   C. the amount of matter in an object.
   D. the pull of gravity on an object.

12. The ability to _____ is NOT a chemical property.

   A. float   C. burn
   B. tarnish   D. rust

13. The metric system is _____.

   A. used only to measure the mass of objects.
   B. used only to measure the height of objects.
   C. not used by scientists.
   D. based on multiples of 10.

14. Air is an example of a _____.

   A. solid.   C. gas.
   B. liquid.   D. property.

Inquiry Skills

15. **Predict** A pot of water is being heated on a stove. Will the physical properties of the water change? Will its chemical properties change? Explain.

16. **Measure** What is the volume of the liquid?

Map the Concept

Use terms from the list to complete the concept map.

Solid
States of Matter
Liquid
Gas

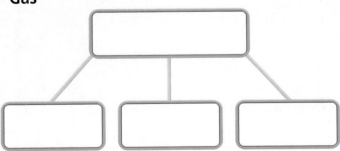

Critical Thinking

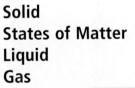

17. **Apply** Compare the mass of an astronaut on Earth with the mass of the same astronaut on the Moon. Then compare the weight of an astronaut on Earth with the weight of the same astronaut on the Moon.

18. **Synthesize** An unknown substance has a volume of 25 mL. It is placed into a different container and its volume changes to 50 mL. What can you conclude about the state of matter of this substance? Explain.

19. **Evaluate** You are given two cubes that are the same size and have the same texture. You are told that the cubes are identical. How could you test to see if this statement is correct?

20. **Analyze** Why is texture a physical property of matter and not a chemical property?

Performance Assessment

Physical Properties
Obtain a block of wood from your teacher. Describe and measure as many physical properties of the block of wood as you can.

Chapter 13

How Matter Changes

LESSON 1

Cut a sheet of paper to make a paper snowflake, or break a piece of candy to make smaller pieces—is the paper still paper, is the candy still candy?

Read about it in Lesson 1.

LESSON 2

From a hot air balloon rising to water boiling in a pot—how does heat change matter?

Read about it in Lesson 2.

LESSON 3

Pure gold is soft, but gold jewelry is hard—how are common mixtures useful?

Read about it in Lesson 3.

LESSON 4

From the exploding lights of fireworks to the glow of fireflies—are chemical changes the cause?

Read about it in Lesson 4.

What Are Physical Changes in Matter?

Why It Matters...

When you cut a piece of paper, you change the way it looks. It would be hard to make the paper look as it did before it was cut. But the paper is still paper. It has not become a new kind of matter.

PREPARE TO INVESTIGATE

Inquiry Skill

Compare When you compare two things, you observe how they are alike and how they are different.

Materials

- 2 clear plastic cups
- 2 saltine crackers
- crushed or shaved ice
- spoon
- metric ruler
- marker

Science and Math Toolbox

For steps 2–4, review **Using a Tape Measure or Ruler** on page H6.

Matter Changes
Procedure

1 In your *Science Notebook*, make a chart like the one shown. Half fill a plastic cup with crushed ice. Put two crackers in another cup.

2 **Measure** Use a metric ruler to measure the height of the crushed ice and of the crackers. Mark the heights on the outside of the cups. Label the marks *Ice* and *Whole Crackers*. Record the height, shape, and state of the materials in your chart.

3 **Compare** Allow the ice to melt. Crush the crackers with a spoon. Measure the height of both materials and mark them on the cups. Label the marks *Melted Ice* and *Crushed Crackers*. Record the height, shape, and state of the materials.

4 Combine the materials in one cup and stir them together. Mark the height and label it *Mixture*. Record the height, shape, and state of the mixture.

STEP 1

Material	Height	Shape	State
Crushed ice			
Whole crackers			
Crushed crackers			
Melted ice			
Mixture			

STEP 3

STEP 4

Conclusion

1. **Analyze Data** How did each material change during each step?

2. **Infer** Were any materials taken away during the experiment? Were any new materials added?

3. **Predict** How do you think the mixture will change if you place it in a freezer?

Investigate More!

Design an Experiment Allow the mixture from step 4 to dry out. Measure the height of the material that remains. Is the height close to the height of any of the materials in the Investigate?

Physical Changes

MAIN IDEA Physical changes involve a change in size, shape, or state. No new kinds of matter are formed. All changes in matter involve energy.

READING SKILL

Cause and Effect On a chart, list three examples of physical changes and the cause of each change.

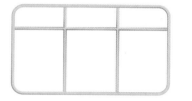

Size, Shape, and State

Suppose you are playing baseball with friends. You hit a home run right through the garage window. The glass shatters into hundreds of tiny pieces. Your baseball has caused a physical change in the window glass. A **physical change** is a change in the way matter looks without changing it into a new kind of matter.

Many physical changes change the size, shape, or state of matter. Breaking the window caused a change in the shape and size of the window glass, but each tiny piece of glass still has the properties of glass. No new kinds of matter were formed.

The shape and size of the candy changes when it is smashed with a hammer. But other properties of the candy stay the same.

▲ The melting juice bar is changing from a solid to a liquid. Changes of state are physical changes.

likely break into smaller pieces as the hard candy did. The hard candy would not melt as easily as the juice bar would. Not all matter changes in the same way when conditions are the same. For example, at 0°C, pure water freezes but salt water does not.

▶ **CAUSE AND EFFECT** How does matter change in a physical change?

The melted part of this juice bar looks different from the frozen part. If you could taste the melted part of the juice bar, you would observe that it tastes the same as the frozen bar. The melted juice bar is not a new kind of matter. It still tastes like a juice bar—it has only changed from a solid to a liquid. A change in state is a physical change.

Suppose you smashed the juice bar with a hammer in the same way as the hard candy in the picture was smashed. How would smashing the juice bar change it? The juice bar would

When this balloon is blown up, it looks bigger, but it is still made of the same kind of matter. A change in size is a physical change. ▶

Common Physical Changes

The art supplies on the table have been cut, molded, and colored. You know that these changes are physical changes because the art supplies have not been changed into something new. A student has cut the paper, molded the clay, and drawn on the paper.

Whenever matter is moved or changed, energy (EHN ur jee) is always involved. **Energy** is the ability to cause change. Sometimes energy must be added to matter to cause a change. For example, a glue stick melts in a hot glue gun when heat is added. Heat is one form of energy.

Sometimes energy is given off by matter when it changes. Suppose a paper clip is quickly bent back and forth several times. The paper clip will feel warmer than it did before it was bent. That is because heat energy is given off.

Think about physical changes that happen around you every day—melting ice, breaking glass, or building a sand castle. These changes in form, size, and shape cannot occur without energy. Heat from the Sun melts ice. The energy of a moving baseball breaks glass. You use energy in your muscles to form sand into a sand castle.

▶ **CAUSE AND EFFECT** What form of energy causes ice to melt?

This student has caused many physical changes while creating this art project.

Visual Summary

A physical change involves a change in size, shape, or state. No new kinds of matter are formed.

All changes in matter involve energy. Energy may be added, or it may be given off.

 for Home and School

MATH **Do Origami** Japanese origami is a way of physically changing a piece of paper into complex shapes by folding it. Find some origami instructions in a book or on the Internet. Try to make some shapes. As you fold, keep a log of geometric shapes that you notice.

ART **Make a Movie** Use flipbook animation to show a physical change to an object. For example, draw a sequence on a pad to show an ice cube melting or a can being crushed. Share your movie with your classmates.

Review

1 MAIN IDEA How do you know that melting ice is a physical change?

2 VOCABULARY Use your own words to describe what energy is.

3 READING SKILL: Cause and Effect What type of energy causes a rain puddle to disappear on a sunny day?

4 CRITICAL THINKING: Analyze A plumber uses a torch to heat a copper pipe in order to bend it. Is this change a physical change? Explain.

5 INQUIRY SKILL: Compare Compare the properties of broken and unbroken glass. Explain why breaking glass is a physical change.

✓ **TEST PREP**
Which of the following is NOT a physical change?

A. A dish of water set out in the Sun becomes dry.

B. Wood burns in a campfire to form charcoal.

C. A sandwich is cut into four smaller pieces.

D. Chocolate melts in your pocket on a hot day.

Technology
Visit **www.eduplace.com/scp/** to find out more about physical changes.

What Happens When Matter Is Heated or Cooled?

Why It Matters...

An iceberg is a large chunk of floating ice in the ocean. Over time, parts of an iceberg melt. Melting ice is water changing state from a solid to a liquid—a physical change. But why does water change form? To find out, you have to look at the particles of matter that make up water.

PREPARE TO INVESTIGATE

Inquiry Skill

Measure When you measure, you use tools to find the height, volume, or distance around an object.

Materials

- 2 small round balloons, inflated
- waterproof marking pen
- metric tape measure
- plastic dishpan
- water
- ice cubes
- clock or watch

Science and Math Toolbox

For steps 2–4, review **Using a Tape Measure or Ruler** on page H6.

Balloon Bath

Procedure

STEP 1

Balloon	Measurement (in/cm)
A original measurement	
A after cooling	
B original measurement	
B after heating	

① **Collaborate** Work with a partner. Make a chart in your *Science Notebook* like the one shown.

② **Measure** Draw a circle around the widest part of each balloon. Write *A* on one balloon and *B* on the other. Measure around each balloon on the lines you made. You can use a string to measure if you need to. Record the measurements.

STEP 2

③ **Experiment** Half fill a dishpan with water and add ice cubes. Place balloon *A* in the ice water. Carefully push the balloon into the water with a ruler.

④ **Record Data** Hold the balloon under the ice water for 3 minutes. Then remove it and quickly measure the distance around the balloon as you did in step 2. Record your measurement.

STEP 3

⑤ **Use Variables** Dump out the ice water and warm the dishpan with warm tap water. Half fill the dishpan with warm tap water.

⑥ **Compare** Repeat step 4 using warm water and balloon *B*.

Conclusion

1. **Analyze Data** How did the balloon change when it was cooled? When it was heated?

2. **Hypothesize** Suggest a reason why the balloons changed size.

Investigate More!

Research Jacques Charles was a French scientist and hot-air balloonist in the late 1700s. Find out about his observations of how temperature affects the volume of a gas.

VOCABULARY

heat	p. E45
temperature	p. E46
thermal energy	p. E44

READING SKILL

Classify Use this chart to classify melting, freezing, boiling, evaporation, and condensation as processes that release or absorb heat.

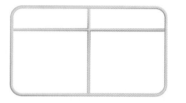

Heating and Cooling Matter

MAIN IDEA Heating and cooling matter changes the motion of its particles and the spacing between them.

Thermal Energy and Matter

Suppose you have a small box and the bottom is packed with marbles. You shake the box gently. The marbles might jiggle, but they don't move and spread out because they are tightly packed in the box. These marbles are like particles in a solid. When the marbles move, they have energy of motion—even if it is just a small amount. You could say that they have very little thermal energy (THUR muhl EHN ur jee). **Thermal energy** is the total energy of the particles of matter. It is related to the energy of the moving particles. The particles of a solid have very little energy of motion.

Liquid Iron

The particles of liquid iron are farther apart than the particles of iron in the solid beam. This change of state occurs because the thermal energy of the iron has been increased.

If you shake the box harder, you add more energy to the marbles. The marbles would break out of their arrangement on the bottom of the box and move farther and faster. This is also true of particles of matter. If you add more energy to matter, its particles move faster and farther apart.

Thermal energy can be added to matter. It can also be taken away from matter. You cannot see thermal energy, but you can feel it as heat. **Heat** (heet) is the flow of thermal energy from a warmer area to a cooler area.

When you add heat to matter, its thermal energy increases. The particles of matter move faster and farther apart. When you cool matter, you remove thermal energy. The particles of matter slow down and move closer together.

When the metal jar lid shown is heated by hot water, its particles

before

after

Thermal energy from the hot water flows to the cooler lid. The particles of the lid gain thermal energy and move faster and farther apart.

move faster and farther apart. The lid expands, or gets larger, and loosens from the jar. Cooling the lid would cause the particles to move more slowly and closer together. The lid would contract, or get tighter.

▶ **CLASSIFY** Classify liquid iron and solid iron as having less thermal energy or more thermal energy.

Solid Iron
The particles of iron in the solid beam are packed tightly and held rigidly in place. They can vibrate, but they cannot move past each other.

3 Because the air particles are farther apart, the heated air inside the balloon is less dense than the cooler air outside the balloon. That is why the balloon rises.

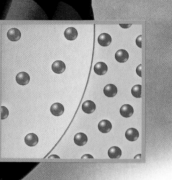

2 Adding heat causes the air particles inside the balloon to move faster and farther apart.

1 The burner heats the air inside the hot-air balloon.

Temperature

On a snowy day, the air outside is much colder than the air inside your house. How much colder? You can find out by measuring the air temperature (TEHM pur uh chur). **Temperature** is a measure of how hot or cold matter is. It also describes how fast the particles of matter are moving. Particles of matter move slower at lower temperatures. Particles move faster at higher temperatures.

A thermometer (thur MAHM-ih tur) is a tool used to measure temperature. Some thermometers are made of a tube filled with liquid. When the air around the tube is heated, the liquid expands and rises in the tube. When the air cools, the liquid contracts and falls in the tube.

Thermometers measure temperature in units called degrees. Scientists and people in other countries use the Celsius (SEHL see uhs) scale. In the United States, temperature is usually measured using the Fahrenheit (FAR uhn hyt) scale.

◄ This photo was taken with an infrared camera that detects heat as areas of red. It shows that thermal energy is moving from parts of the house to the cooler outside air. The outside air becomes warmer, as the inside air gets cooler.

Any action that adds heat to an object will raise its temperature. When you cook, you are adding heat to food. The food absorbs heat, becomes warmer, and has a higher temperature. To make your cold hands feel warmer, you can rub them together. When you quickly bend a paper clip back and forth, it begins to feel warm.

How can the temperature of an object be lowered? Remember that heat is the flow of thermal energy from a warmer area to a cooler area. The temperature of an object can be lowered simply by putting the object in a cooler place. In a refrigerator or freezer, the air is colder than the object, so heat is released by the object into the cold air.

► CLASSIFY What are two scales people use to measure temperature?

The temperature on the thermometer shows 0°C and 32°F. Why is the boy dressed warmly? ►

Changes in State

Matter can be a solid, liquid, or gas depending on its temperature. When matter is heated or cooled, its temperature changes, and it changes state. Melting, freezing, boiling, and condensation are physical changes in the state of matter.

The arrangement of particles in matter varies. Particles in a solid are held in place and cannot move past each other. In a liquid, the particles can move past each other, but they are still close together. The particles in a gas move quickly and there is much space between them.

Change State

Original State of Matter	Change	Resulting State of Matter
Solid	**Melting** Adding thermal energy to turn a solid into a liquid	Liquid
Liquid	**Freezing** Removing thermal energy to turn a liquid into a solid	Solid
Liquid	**Boiling** Adding thermal energy to turn a liquid into a gas	Gas
Gas	**Condensation** A gas or vapor cools and becomes a liquid	Liquid

What change in state is happening to the ice? Are the particles of water gaining thermal energy or losing thermal energy?

When heat is added to matter, the particles of matter move faster and farther apart. Adding heat to a solid causes the particles to move faster and faster until they break free of their positions. The solid melts and becomes liquid. If the liquid is heated, its particles move faster and faster until they spread even farther apart. The liquid evaporates and becomes a gas. The higher the temperature, the faster the liquid evaporates. Boiling is very rapid evaporation.

These changes in state can be reversed simply by removing heat from matter. Removing heat makes the particles of matter move more slowly and closer together. As matter cools, gases condense to form liquids, and liquids freeze to form solids.

Changes in state are physical changes because the appearance of matter changes, but a new kind of matter has not formed. In changes of state, matter looks different because the particles of matter are arranged differently.

The particles themselves have not changed. The particles of ice are the same as the particles of liquid water—they differ only in the way that they are arranged.

You have probably noticed that different kinds of matter are found in different states at the same temperature. The particles that make up different kinds of matter have different properties. At room temperature, for example, the particles of a solid are held together more strongly than the particles of a liquid. The particles of a gas have little or no attraction between them. Particles that are held together strongly need more energy to break them apart.

▶ **CLASSIFY** **Classify the four types of physical changes by whether thermal energy is added or removed.**

Matter Stays the Same

Although the appearance of matter might change in a physical change, the kind of matter itself does not change. Its physical properties, such as color and density, stay the same. Its mass, or amount of matter, also stays the same. For example, when 100 g of ice melt, the mass of water that forms will also equal 100 g.

Water is not the only kind of matter that changes state. Metals, such as iron, can change state, too. When iron is heated, it gets soft. Softened metals can be hammered and bent into different shapes, as you can see in the picture. When more heat is added, the metal gets even softer. Finally, it melts.

▶ **CAUSE AND EFFECT** **How is the mass of an object affected when the object changes state?**

Philip Simmons is a well-known ironworker and metal artist in Charleston, South Carolina. He uses thermal energy to change the shape of iron to create beautiful wrought-iron gates, such as the one below.

Visual Summary

Thermal energy is the total energy of the particles of matter.

Particles of matter move faster when heated and slower when cooled.

Temperature measures how hot or cold matter is and describes how fast its particles are moving.

 **for Home and School**

WRITING Narrative Today, nearly every kitchen in America has a refrigerator. But it wasn't always that way. Find out what life was like before refrigeration. Then use your imagination to write a story about what life was like during that time.

TECHNOLOGY Make a "How It Works" Poster An air conditioner keeps a building cool. It works by using the transfer of thermal energy and the physical properties of liquids and gases. Research to find out how air conditioners work. Make a poster that includes diagrams, labels, and explanations.

Review

1 MAIN IDEA How does heating affect particles of matter?

2 VOCABULARY How is thermal energy related to heat?

3 READING SKILL: Classify Classify each of the following changes according to whether they are caused by adding heat or removing heat: boiling, condensation, melting, freezing.

4 CRITICAL THINKING: Apply Which do you think would boil sooner when heated—a cup of cold water or a cup of warm water? Explain your answer.

5 INQUIRY SKILL: Measure What tool would you use to measure the outside air temperature?

TEST PREP
Which occurs when heat is removed from an object?

A. The particles of the object move faster and farther apart.

B. The object expands.

C. The particles of the object gain thermal energy.

D. The particles of the object move slower and closer together.

Technology
Visit **www.eduplace.com/scp/** to learn more about thermal energy.

What Are Mixtures and Solutions?

Why It Matters...

When you shake a snow globe, solid and liquid matter mix together. But the different kinds of matter do not change into something new. You can see this when you watch it "snow." The different kinds of matter separate from each other.

PREPARE TO INVESTIGATE

Inquiry Skill

Compare When you compare two things, you observe how they are alike and how they are different.

Materials

- 4 plastic cups
- marking pen
- water
- spoon
- fine sand
- table salt
- hand lens
- goggles

Science and Math Toolbox

For step 4, review **Using a Hand Lens** on page H2.

Making Mixtures
Procedure

1. **Collaborate** Work with a partner. Make a chart in your *Science Notebook* like the one shown.

2. Use a marking pen to label four cups *Water*, *Sand*, *Salt*, and *Both*. Half-fill each cup with water.

3. **Experiment** Add a $\frac{1}{2}$ spoonful of sand to the cup labeled *Sand*, a $\frac{1}{2}$ spoonful of salt to the cup labeled *Salt*, and a $\frac{1}{2}$ spoonful of both sand and salt to the cup labeled *Both*. Stir the contents of all four cups. **Safety:** Wear goggles when handling sand.

4. **Observe** Examine the liquid in each cup with a hand lens. Record your observations in your chart.

Conclusion

1. **Communicate** What happened to the mixture in each cup when you stirred it?

2. **Compare** In what way did the mixtures in the cups look the same when viewed with the hand lens? In what way did they look different?

3. **Predict** Suggest a way you could separate the sand, the salt, and the water in the cup labeled *Both*.

4. **Use Variables** What was the purpose of the cup labeled *Water*?

STEP 1

Cup	Observations
Water	
Sand	
Salt	
Both	

STEP 3

STEP 4

Investigate More!

Design an Experiment
Use your answer to Conclusion 3 to design an experiment that will separate sand, salt, and water mixed together. With permission, carry out the experiment.

VOCABULARY

dissolve   p. E58
mixture   p. E54
solution   p. E58

READING SKILL

Text Structure Make an outline of the lesson using the headings. In which part of the lesson will you learn about solutions?

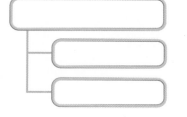

Mixtures and Solutions

MAIN IDEA Mixtures and solutions are made up of two or more substances that are combined in a physical change.

Mixtures

What's at the bottom of your backpack? Maybe you have a combination of broken pencils, erasers, paper clips, and scraps of paper. This combination of things is a mixture. A **mixture** is matter made up of two or more substances that are combined physically. Making a mixture is a physical change. Although the pencils, erasers, paper clips, and scraps of paper are all mixed up, their physical properties have not changed. The pencils are still pencils. The paper clips are still paper clips.

This mixture of iron filings and sand is easy to separate using a magnet. Because making a mixture is a physical change, the parts of a mixture keep their properties.

You can easily separate the mixture at the bottom of your backpack by using differences in physical properties. The more different the properties of the parts are, the easier it is to separate the parts. Separating the parts of a mixture is also a physical change.

Not all mixtures can be separated by hand. Some mixtures can be separated using a change in state. To separate a mixture of sugar and water, you could boil it. The water would change to a gas, leaving the sugar behind.

Differences in density can also be used to separate a mixture. Remember that like mass and volume, density is a physical property of matter. A sample of soil can be divided into its parts by mixing it with water and allowing the mixture to settle. The most dense soil parts sink first. The least dense parts sink later. The soil might divide into a dense layer of small stones on the bottom, followed by a layer of sand, then a layer of clay, with water at the top.

▶ **TEXT STRUCTURE** **What is the main idea of this lesson? How do you know?**

▲ **What physical properties of the parts of this mixture are being used to separate it?**

This device can separate a mixture of coins according to their size. ▶

Some Common Mixtures

When you last blew bubbles, did you know that you were playing with a mixture? Look around. You will find mixtures everywhere. The water you drink has minerals mixed up in it. A bowl of soup and a glass of milk are both mixtures. A trombone is made of brass, a mixture of metals. Your drawer full of socks is a mixture, and so is a bag of trail mix. Mixtures can be any combination of matter. They can be combinations of solids only, liquids only, gases only, or a combination of any of the three.

In some mixtures, like soup, it is easy to see the separate parts. Not every spoonful of soup is the same. Some spoonfuls might have many carrots. Other spoonfuls might have only noodles. It is easy to see that the separate parts of soup have not lost their physical properties.

In other mixtures, you cannot see the separate parts. In lemonade, you cannot see the water, lemon juice, and sugar that make up the mixture. Every sip of lemonade has the same taste. One sip is not sweeter than another. Although it is not easy to see, the separate parts of lemonade still have their own physical properties.

Although you cannot see the separate parts, these bubbles are a mixture of soap and water.

Look for mixtures in this lighthouse scene. Some mixtures are easier to see than others. You might have guessed that fog is a mixture of air and water. Air is a mixture of gases. Another mixture you might recognize is sea water. Sea water is a mixture of water and salts. Rock is a mixture of minerals. The lighthouse is made of many different mixtures. Concrete is a mixture of gravel, sand, limestone, clay, and water. The glass and the metal that make up the light are both mixtures. Even the paint on the lighthouse is a mixture.

▶ **TEXT STRUCTURE** **Where in the text would you find examples of common mixtures?**

It is easy to see the separate parts of the glittery mixture inside the wand. ▼

Fog is a mixture of air and water. Air is a mixture of gases, including nitrogen, oxygen, and carbon dioxide. ▼

Solutions

A mixture of sand and water looks different from a mixture of salt and water. You can see the particles of sand in the sand and water mixture, but the particles of salt seem to have disappeared in the salt and water mixture. If you taste salt water, you know that the salt is still there. Salt water is a special mixture called a solution (suh LOO shuhn). A **solution** is a mixture in which the particles of one kind of matter are mixed evenly with the particles of other kinds of matter. A solution has the same properties throughout because its different parts are evenly mixed.

Because you can taste the salt in salt water, you know that the salt is still there. You cannot see the salt because it has dissolved. To **dissolve** means to mix completely by separating into particles that cannot be seen.

Components of Sea Water

Dissolved Salts	
Chlorine	55.0%
Sodium	30.6%
Sulfate	7.7%
Magnesium	3.7%
Calcium	1.2%
Potassium	1.1%
Other	0.7%

Water 96.5%

Dissolved Salts 3.5%

Sea water is the most common liquid solution on Earth. For every 1,000 g of sea water, there are 965 g of water. Dissolved in the water are 35 g of salts.

As salt dissolves in water, the particles of salt are surrounded by particles of water. The water particles and salt particles are attracted to each other. Eventually, the solid salt is completely broken down into particles that are evenly mixed with water particles. The salt becomes invisible.

What happens if you keep adding salt to the salt water solution? After a while, the salt will no longer dissolve because there are more salt particles than the water can hold. The extra salt will settle to the bottom of the container.

Remember the bubble mixture? This mixture is a solution, too. Particles of soap are pulled apart by water particles. They spread throughout the liquid and become completely mixed. The parts of a solution cannot be separated by hand. No matter how long you wait, the particles of soap will not sink to the bottom.

Although the properties of a solution are often different from the properties of its separate parts, dissolving is a physical change. The physical properties of the parts of the solution stay the same.

A solution can also be separated into its parts. When the water evaporates from a salt water solution, the salt is left behind.

▶ TEXT STRUCTURE What is a title that could be used for the photograph and caption at the bottom of this page?

These crystals of table salt contain millions of particles of salt. When the crystals are added to water, the salt particles spread out in the water and become evenly mixed with the water particles.

Sand is not soluble in water. No particles of sand are dissolved in this beaker of water.

Salt is more soluble in water than sand. Some salt has settled to the bottom of the beaker.

Sugar is very soluble in water. All the sugar that has been added to the water has dissolved.

Comparing Solutions

Compare the mixtures in the beakers above. The same amount of solid was added to equal amounts of water. Some solids dissolve in water better than others. Solubility (sahl yuh BIHL ih tee) is a measure of how much of a substance can dissolve in another substance. The solubility of a substance depends on the temperature and the substance in which it is dissolving.

Look again at the three beakers. If you add sand to a beaker of water at room temperature, all the sand settles to the bottom. Sand is not soluble in water. Sand particles cannot separate and mix with

particles of water. Salt and sugar are both soluble in water at room temperature. However, you can see that sugar is more soluble than salt. In fact, you can dissolve five times more sugar than salt in an equal amount of water.

Because solutions are mixtures, it does not matter exactly how much of each part is mixed together. A solution of salt water can have a lot of salt and taste very salty. It can also have only a little salt and taste slightly salty. Both mixtures are still solutions of salt water.

▶ **MAIN IDEA** What is solubility?

Visual Summary

In a mixture, two or more kinds of matter combine, but their properties do not change.

In a solution, the particles of different kinds of matter are evenly mixed together.

Different substances have different solubilities.

LINKS for Home and School

MATH **Converting Units** You can dissolve 35.9 g of salt in 100 mL of water at room temperature. If you add any more salt to the solution, it will not dissolve. Suppose you pour 450 g of salt into 1 L of water. How much salt will dissolve? How much will not dissolve?

SOCIAL STUDIES **Tell About the Dead Sea** If water is salty enough, you can float on it. The Dead Sea is the saltiest body of water in the world. It is so salty that no fish can live in it! It is also a popular travel destination and an important historical site. Do some research on the Dead Sea. Give an oral presentation on what you learn.

Review

1 MAIN IDEA How is a mixture made?

2 VOCABULARY What is a solution? Give an example of a solution.

3 READING SKILL: Text Structure Identify and describe the sequence of dissolving.

4 CRITICAL THINKING: Analyze Why do you think it is easier to separate a mixture of two liquids with very different boiling points than two liquids with almost the same boiling points?

5 INQUIRY SKILL: Compare Vegetable soup and tomato juice are both mixtures. Describe how these mixtures are alike and different.

TEST PREP
Which of the following is a solution?

A. soil

B. rocks

C. lemonade

D. noodle soup

Technology
Visit **www.eduplace.com/scp/** to learn more about mixtures and solutions.

First Snow

A Native American Myth

A Native American myth tells the story of a mischievous Coyote who gave snow to the First People of the World. But the People didn't know what to do with the beautiful, white powder. Coyote had to teach them. Read the excerpt below from the story "First Snow," from *The Golden Hoard* by Geraldine McCaughrean.

Coyote had filled a cooking pot with white handfuls from a drift of snow. He lit a fire and smoke curled up into the sky, fraying it to gray. He began to cook the snow. The People crowded around to see what delicious stew he was making. But as they watched, they began to shiver.

First the snow in the pot turned gray, then to transparent liquid, seething, bubbling, boiling and steaming, cooling only as the fire burned out. As it did so, the snow on the trees wept and dripped and dropped down in icy tears. The white on the ground changed to a gray slush that soaked

the children's moccasins, and the women let fall their skirtfuls of snow, crying, "Oh! Urgh! So cold! So wet! Urgh! Oh!" The old people drew their shawls about their heads and shook their wet mittens....

"Now look what you've done!" cried First Woman, wrapping herself tight in a dozen shawls. "Our lovely food has rotted away and there's nothing left but the juices. What a wicked waste! You always were a troublemaker, Coyote! In the time before the world, you were always making mischief, stealing, tricking, complaining. But this is the worst! You've made all our beautiful sky flour melt away!"

The People tried to pelt him with snowballs, but the snow only turned to water in their palms.

Coyote simply drank from the pot of melted snow, then shook his head so hard that his yellow ears rattled.

"You don't understand," he said gently. "Snow was not meant for food. It was sent down upon the five mountaintops for the springtime sun to melt, drip joining drop, dribble joining trickle, stream joining river, filling the lakes and pools and ponds, before it rolls down to the sea. Now, when you are thirsty, you need not wait for the rain, or catch the raindrops in your hands. You can drink whenever you please."

Sharing Ideas

1. **READING CHECK** Why does Coyote give snow to the People of the World?

2. **WRITE ABOUT IT** Imagine you are seeing snow for the first time. Write a journal entry describing what it is like.

3. **TALK ABOUT IT** Discuss the changes of state that occurred to water in this story.

What Are Chemical Changes in Matter?

Why It Matters...

How does a hard, green, tasteless strawberry become ripe, red, and sweet? The answer lies in the changes that take place within the the strawberry. Sugars and flavors—new kinds of matter—are produced during some of these changes. This is what makes the strawberry taste so good.

PREPARE TO INVESTIGATE

Inquiry Skill

Observe It is important to know the difference between what you observe with your senses and instruments and what you think about those observations.

Materials

- vinegar
- measuring tablespoon
- plastic cup
- thermometer
- measuring teaspoon
- baking soda
- goggles

Science and Math Toolbox

For steps 3 and 5, review **Using a Thermometer** on page H8.

A Cool Change

Procedure

1 **Collaborate** Work with a partner. Make a chart in your *Science Notebook* like the one shown.

2 **Measure** Put four tablespoons of vinegar in a cup. **Safety:** Wear goggles.

3 **Measure** Use a thermometer to find the temperature of the vinegar. Record this starting temperature in your chart.

4 **Observe** Measure one-half teaspoon of baking soda and add it to the vinegar. Record your observations in your chart.

5 **Record Data** When the change stops, measure the temperature of the liquid in the cup as you did in step 3. Record this final temperature in your chart.

Conclusion

1. **Communicate** Describe what happened after you added baking soda to the cup.

2. **Analyze Data** How did the temperature change after you added baking soda?

3. **Hypothesize** What do you think happened to the baking soda after you added it to the cup? What observations led you to make this hypothesis?

STEP 1

Starting temperature	
Observations of vinegar and baking soda	
Final temperature	

STEP 3

STEP 4

Investigate More!

Design an Experiment
Did the properties of the vinegar change? Try adding more and more baking soda to the liquid from step 5. Do you get the same reaction? Is this a physical change?

Chemical Changes

VOCABULARY

chemical change p. E66
chemical reaction p. E67
product   p. E67
reactant   p. E67

READING SKILL

Cause and Effect Use the diagram to show that a bonfire releases energy and forms new kinds of matter.

Burning is a chemical change that gives off light and heat, which are two forms of energy. ▼

MAIN IDEA A chemical change produces new kinds of matter.

New Matter

Waffles for breakfast! If you've ever made batter for waffles, you know that it is a mixture that includes flour, sugar, oil, and eggs. Can you taste the eggs when you eat a waffle? Not usually. After you cook waffle batter, it looks different from the way it looked before. The properties of the flour, sugar, oil, and eggs have also changed. That is why you cannot taste the eggs. Cooking waffle batter is not a physical change. It is a chemical change.

A **chemical change** is a change in matter that produces new kinds of matter with different properties. Energy is always involved in a chemical change. It is either given off or taken in. When you make waffles, energy is taken in by the batter to produce a new kind of matter.

In a chemical reaction, the properties of the products (waffles) are always different from the properties of the reactants (the ingredients in the waffle batter).

Like physical changes, chemical changes involve particles of matter—atoms and molecules. In a chemical change, however, atoms and molecules do not simply rearrange. Molecules break apart and form new combinations with other atoms and molecules. The result is new matter with different properties. Atoms and molecules form these new combinations in a chemical reaction (ree AK shuhn). A **chemical reaction** is another term for a chemical change.

In a chemical reaction, the matter that you start with is called the **reactant** (ree AK tuhnt). When you make waffles, the reactants include flour, sugar, oil, and eggs. The **product** of a chemical reaction is the newly formed matter. Waffles are the product when cooking waffle batter.

▶ CAUSE AND EFFECT What happens to matter during a chemical reaction?

Common Chemical Changes

Every time you ride in a car, you depend on chemical changes. First, a chemical reaction in the car battery produces electricity that starts the car. Then the car engine burns gasoline in a chemical reaction to produce energy that moves the car. The exhaust includes the products of burning gasoline.

Chemical changes happen all around you. Burning wood, exploding fireworks, and rusting metal are chemical changes. Your body changes food in chemical reactions to give you the molecules and energy you need to grow.

Clues that a chemical change is taking place include bubbles and changes in color, state, temperature, odor, and energy. Thermal energy is the most common form of energy involved in chemical changes. Thermal energy can be added, such as when lighting a fire, or released, such as in an explosion.

Other forms of energy involved in chemical changes include light, electricity, sound, and motion. The biggest clue to a chemical change is the formation of products that have properties different from those of the reactants.

Chemical Change in a Battery

Case The plastic case keeps the chemicals inside the battery.

The chemical reaction that takes place in a car battery releases energy in the form of electricity. This electrical energy is used to start the car.

Terminals Electrical energy flows in and out of the battery through wires connected to the terminals.

Cells Compartments in the battery contain lead, lead oxide, and acid.

Antacid and Water

Bubbles Carbon dioxide gas is produced by the reaction.

The formation of bubbles is a clue that a chemical reaction is taking place.

Tablet This antacid tablet contains citric acid and baking soda.

Liquid The reaction absorbs heat from the water, and the temperature of the water decreases.

How does a chemical change occur? Atoms in molecules are held together by forces of attraction called chemical bonds. During a chemical reaction, the bonds that hold these particles together are broken. New bonds form between atoms, resulting in new molecules and new products. These new products have different properties from the reactants. This is because the products are made up of a different combination of atoms and molecules.

Energy is often given off when a chemical reaction takes place. This release of energy can be very helpful when heating a house, starting a car, or lighting up a dark place. Sometimes this release of energy can be dangerous. An explosion can destroy buildings and injure people.

▶ **CAUSE AND EFFECT** What happens when new chemical bonds are formed?

When two reactants are mixed together in a glow stick, a reaction occurs that produces light but very little heat. ▶

Comparing Physical and Chemical Changes

You have learned that matter can change physically and chemically. In a physical change, no new kind of matter is formed. Although matter might look different, the chemical bonds between the particles of matter have not been broken.

A chemical change always produces a new kind of matter. The new matter looks different and has different physical properties. This is because the chemical bonds between the particles of reactants have been broken and reformed. Compare the physical and chemical changes in the table.

Comparing Changes in Matter

Physical Changes	Chemical Changes
Grinding up a sugar cube does not change the kind of matter. Tiny pieces of sugar are still sugar.	Caramel is burned sugar. Heat changes some of the sugar particles into carbon and water.
Folding paper does not break chemical bonds. No new bonds are formed. Folded paper is still paper.	When paper is burned, carbon in the paper combines with oxygen to form ash and carbon dioxide gas.
Copper can be bent easily. Bending a copper tube does not break bonds. Copper is still copper.	When copper is exposed to moist air, it reacts with gases in the air to form a green coating.

Do you like toasted marshmallows best when they are soft and warm or brown and crunchy? Either way you like them, you probably know that it takes longer to toast marshmallows to a deep brown. It takes more heat from the fire—more energy—to brown a marshmallow than to simply make it softer. It often takes more energy to cause a chemical change than to cause a physical change.

It also takes energy to separate physical and chemical combinations. A physical combination is a mixture like sugar water. A chemical combination, or chemical compound, is a combination of atoms that are held together by chemical bonds. Sugar is a chemical compound. To separate sugar water, you can allow the water to evaporate into the air. Energy from the sun causes the water to evaporate. To separate the atoms in sugar, though, you must heat it to very high temperatures— high enough to break the chemical bonds between the three kinds of atoms that make up sugar.

▶ **CAUSE AND EFFECT** What causes chemical bonds in sugar molecules to break apart?

Toasting a marshmallow begins as a physical change. At a certain temperature, the bonds in the sugar molecules of the marshmallow begin to break apart. The marshmallow turns brown. At this point, a chemical change occurs.

Visual Summary

Cause
Chemical Change

↓

Effects
- Energy change
- Color change
- Odor change
- Gas or solid formed
- Bonds broken and new bonds formed

LINKS for Home and School

MATH **Put Wood in Order** Usually, the more dense firewood is, the longer it will burn. Density is usually described as mass per volume with grams per cubic centimeter. Here are some wood densities: Oak 0.59 g/cm³; Elm 0.60 g/cm³; Apple 0.66 g/cm³; Maple 0.76 g/cm³; Pine 0.53 g/cm³. Put the different types of wood in order of density from lowest to highest. Which wood is likely to burn the longest?

WRITING **Story** Write a "Sherlock Holmes"style mystery story involving a chemical reaction. The reaction can be the source of the mystery. The detective can also use a chemical reaction to solve the mystery or catch a villain.

Review

❶ **MAIN IDEA** How are new kinds of matter formed in a chemical change?

❷ **VOCABULARY** What is a reactant? What is one reactant involved in cooking waffles?

❸ **READING SKILL: Cause and Effect** Name some clues that identify baking cookies as a chemical change.

❹ **CRITICAL THINKING: Synthesize** Explain why energy is needed to break bonds.

❺ **INQUIRY SKILL: Observe** When you add vinegar to baking soda, you watch it bubble over and feel the container get slightly cooler. Is this a chemical or physical change? Explain.

✓ TEST PREP

Which of the following is a chemical change?

A. bending a paper clip

B. mixing water and salt

C. rusting iron

D. freezing water

Technology
Visit **www.eduplace.com/scp/** to learn more about chemical changes.

Careers in Science

Fire Investigator

It's a fire investigator's job to figure out exactly how and why a fire started. Fire investigators work at the scene of a fire. They observe damage, take photographs, collect evidence, and interview witnesses. Then they test materials in a lab and write reports on their findings.

What It Takes!

- A degree in fire science
- Skills in problem solving and an interest in chemistry
- Experience as a firefighter

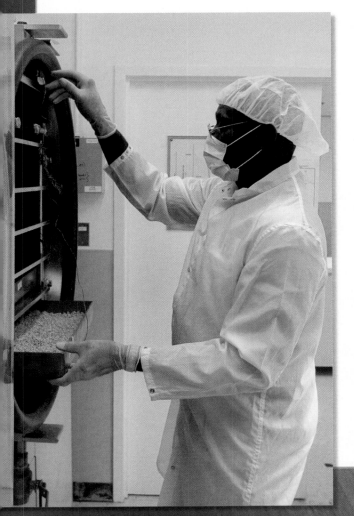

Food Science Technician

Food science technicians work in labs where food is tested for quality and safety. They test to see that nutrition labels on food are correct. They check the taste and smell of the food. They use microscopes to check food for organisms that could cause disease.

Food science technicians need good listening and speaking skills. Many of these technicians work as assistants to food scientists.

What It Takes!

- A high-school diploma
- Additional job-related courses
- An interest in working in a laboratory

LIGHTNING FOSSILS

Lightning is hot! How hot? Would you believe hot enough to melt sand instantly into glass? The temperature of a lightning bolt can reach 50,000°F. That's five times hotter than the Sun's surface!

As it tunnels through the soil, lightning can melt and fuse sand to form a glassy tube called a fulgurite. This odd-sounding name comes from the Latin word "fulgurate," which means lightning.

Fulgurites are usually hollow and very fragile. The longest known fulgurite had three branches totaling 38 feet.

	Temp. (°F)
Human Body	98.6
Boiling Water	212
Clothes Iron	450
Molten Lava	2,000
Sun's Surface	10,000
Lightning Bolt	50,000

As you can see in the chart, the temperature of lightning is 25 times hotter than lava. No wonder it melts sand!

People sometimes call fulgurites "lightning fossils," because they are a kind of physical record or imprint of a lightning bolt in the earth.

Vocabulary

Complete each sentence with a term from the list.

1. When substances _____, they mix completely by separating into particles that can't be seen.

2. A change in the way matter looks but that does not result in a new kind of matter is a/an _____.

3. In a chemical reaction, the newly formed matter is the _____.

4. Matter that is made up of two or more substances that are combined physically is a/an _____.

5. A mixture in which the particles of matter are evenly mixed together is a/an _____.

6. The ability to cause change is called _____.

7. The energy of moving particles in matter is _____.

8. When you measure how hot or cold matter is, you measure _____.

9. The flow of thermal energy from a warmer area to a cooler area is _____.

10. Another term for a chemical change is a/an _____.

chemical change E66
chemical reaction E67
dissolve E58
energy E40
heat E45
mixture E54
physical change E38
product E67
reactant E67
solution E58
temperature E46
thermal energy E44

Test Prep

Write the letter of the best answer choice.

11. When the thermal energy of a particle increases, the particle _____.

    A. moves faster.
    B. moves slower.
    C. moves at the same speed.
    D. doesn't move.

12. When you make waffles, flour is a _____.

    A. chemical change.   **C.** solution.
    B. physical change.   **D.** reactant.

13. An example of a solution is _____.

    A. sea water.
    B. vegetable soup.
    C. sand and water.
    D. concrete.

14. During a chemical change, _____ are broken and reformed.

    A. molecules   **C.** reactants
    B. forms of energy   **D.** products

15. **Compare** Maria pounded an iron nail with a hammer and found that it was still attracted to a magnet. She left that nail to rust and found that it was no longer attracted to the magnet. Describe how the changes to the iron nail were alike and different.

16. **Observe** Chris mixed warm water and hot chocolate mix together. What observations should he make to decide whether the change that occured was a chemical or physical change?

Map the Concept

Use the following terms and phrases to fill in the blanks in the diagram:

Boiling
Physical Changes
Rusting
Dissolving
New Matter Formed
Burning

Critical Thinking

17. **Applying** Compare the energy changes and their effects on particle motion when an ice cube melts and when water vapor condenses.

18. **Synthesizing** A silver spoon that has turned black can be made shiny again by rubbing off the black tarnish with silver polish. Is polishing a physical change or a chemical change? Explain.

19. **Evaluating** A friend tells you that baked cookies are exactly the same matter as the dough used to make them. Evaluate this statement.

20. **Analyzing** Why might water droplets form on the outside of a glass of lemonade?

Performance Assessment

Write a Story
Suppose you are a particle of matter. Write a story describing how you react to changes in your environment, such as temperature changes. What happens when you meet a particle of a substance with which you react? When your story is finished, go back and underline any changes your particle undergoes. Decide whether the changes are physical or chemical.

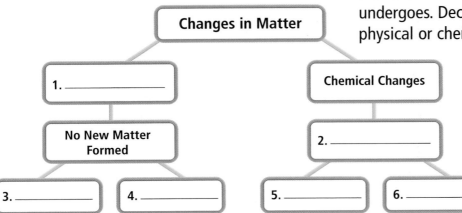

Changes in Matter

1. _____

No New Matter Formed

3. _____   4. _____

Chemical Changes

2. _____

5. _____   6. _____

Write the letter of the best answer choice.

1. Which is NOT a physical change in matter?
   A. melting
   B. breaking
   C. freezing
   D. rusting

2. Which involves a physical change?
   A. baking a cake
   B. boiling water
   C. burning wood
   D. toasting a marshmallow

3. The glass shown contains the labeled substances.

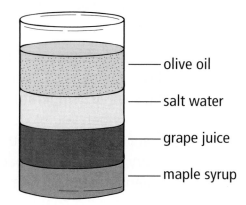

   olive oil
   salt water
   grape juice
   maple syrup

   Which substance is the least dense?
   A. grape juice
   B. maple syrup
   C. olive oil
   D. salt water

4. Which metric unit could be used to measure the mass of a soccer ball?
   A. meters
   B. milliliters
   C. kilograms
   D. cubic centimeters

5. Which is a chemical property of matter?
   A. color
   B. texture
   C. ability to burn
   D. ability to change state

6. A mixture of soil is separated into its parts by adding water and allowing the parts to settle. The mixture separates because the parts differ in _____ .
   A. color.
   B. size.
   C. state.
   D. density.

7. The beakers shown contain equal amounts of water and another material. Which list shows the solubility of the different materials in the beakers, from most to least soluble?

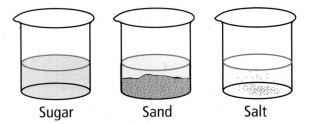

Sugar   Sand   Salt

A. salt, sand, sugar
B. salt, sugar, sand
C. sand, salt, sugar
D. sugar, salt, sand

8. Which of the following is NOT a mixture?
A. fog
B. air
C. soil
D. sugar

Answer the following in complete sentences.

9. How could you measure the volume of a small, irregular solid object, such as the rock shown below?

10. On a hot day, a student observes water drops on the outside of a bottle of cold water. Explain this observation in terms of the concept of thermal energy.

Discover!

A powerful fan fills a hot-air balloon with air. A gas burner heats the air, and the balloon lifts off. The balloon rises because the hot air inside it is lighter and less dense than the air around it. Whether it's in your classroom, in the atmosphere, or in a balloon, hot air always rises.

A burner changes the chemical energy in a fuel, such as propane gas, to thermal energy. The thermal energy flows to the air inside the balloon, making the air warm.

As they get warmer, air particles inside the balloon move faster and farther apart. This makes the hot air inside the balloon lighter and less dense than the cool air outside.

The hot air rises, carrying the balloon with it. Because the burner continues to heat the air inside the balloon, the balloon stays afloat.

To bring the balloon down, the pilot lets some of the hot air out through a vent near the top of the balloon. Cold air enters the balloon from the bottom. With less and less hot air to lift it, the weight of the balloon causes it to sink to the ground.

Fly a hot-air balloon into the air. Go to **www.eduplace.com/scp/** to see how density keeps a balloon afloat.

Science and Math Toolbox

Using a Hand Lens **H2**

Making a Bar Graph **H3**

Using a Calculator **H4**

Finding an Average **H5**

Using a Tape Measure or Ruler **H6**

Measuring Volume **H7**

Using a Thermometer **H8**

Using a Balance **H9**

Making a Chart to Organize Data **H10**

Reading a Circle Graph **H11**

Measuring Elapsed Time **H12**

Measurements **H14**

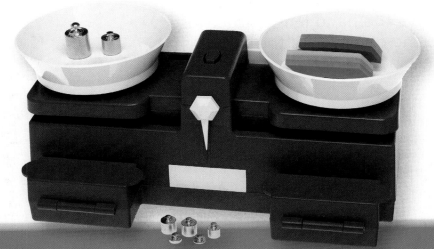

Using a Hand Lens

A hand lens is a tool that magnifies objects, or makes objects appear larger. This makes it possible for you to see details of an object that would be hard to see without the hand lens.

Look at a Coin or a Stamp

1 Place an object such as a coin or a stamp on a table or other flat surface.

STEP 1

2 Hold the hand lens just above the object. As you look through the lens, slowly move the lens away from the object. Notice that the object appears to get larger and a little blurry.

STEP 2

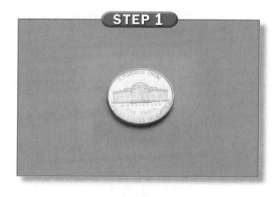

3 Move the hand lens a little closer to the object until the object is once again in sharp focus.

STEP 3

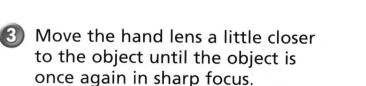

Making a Bar Graph

A bar graph helps you organize and compare data.

Make a Bar Graph of Animal Heights

Animals come in all different shapes and sizes. You can use the information in this table to make a bar graph of animal heights.

1 Draw the side and the bottom of the graph. Label the side of the graph as shown. The numbers will show the height of the animals in centimeters.

2 Label the bottom of the graph. Write the names of the animals at the bottom so that there is room to draw the bars.

3 Choose a title for your graph. Your title should describe the subject of the graph.

4 Draw bars to show the height of each animal. Some heights are between two numbers.

Heights of Animals

Animal	Height (cm)
Bear	240
Elephant	315
Cow	150
Giraffe	570
Camel	210
Horse	165

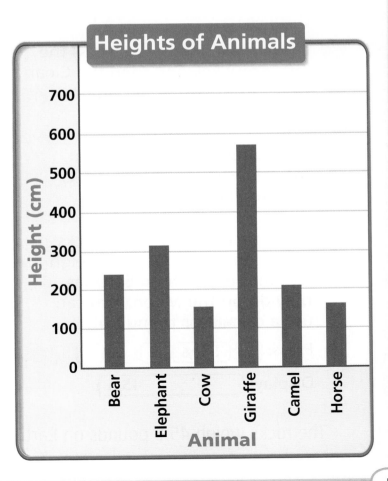

Heights of Animals

Using a Calculator

After you've made measurements, a calculator can help you analyze your data.

Add and Multiply Decimals

Suppose you're an astronaut. You may take 8 pounds of Moon rocks back to Earth. Can you take all the rocks in the table? Use a calculator to find out.

	Weight of Moon Rocks	
Moon Rock	**Weight of Rock on Moon (lb)**
Rock 1	1.7
Rock 2	1.8
Rock 3	2.6
Rock 4	1.5

1 To add, press:

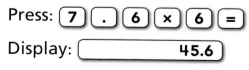

Display: 7.6

2 If you make a mistake, press the left arrow key and then the Clear key. Enter the number again. Then continue adding.

3 Your total is 7.6 pounds. You can take the four Moon rocks back to Earth.

4 How much do the Moon rocks weigh on Earth? Objects weigh six times as much on Earth as they do on the Moon. You can use a calculator to multiply.

Press: 7 . 6 × 6 =

Display: 45.6

The rocks weigh 45.6 pounds on Earth.

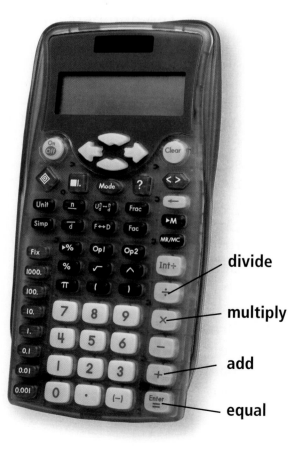

divide

multiply

add

equal

Finding an Average

An average is a way to describe a group of numbers. For example, after you have made a series of measurements, you can find the average. This can help you analyze your data.

Add and Divide to Find the Average

The table shows the amount of rain that fell each month for the first six months of the year. What was the average rainfall per month?

1 Add the numbers in the list.

$$\left.\begin{array}{r} 102 \\ 75 \\ 46 \\ 126 \\ 51 \\ + \ \ 32 \\ \hline 432 \end{array}\right\} \text{6 addends}$$

2 Divide the sum (432) by the number of addends (6).

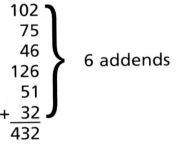

Rainfall	
Month	**Rain (mm)**
January	102
February	75
March	46
April	126
May	51
June	32

The average rainfall per month for the first six months was 72 mm of rain.

Using a Tape Measure or Ruler

Tape measures and rulers are tools for measuring the length of objects and distances. Scientists most often use units such as meters, centimeters, and millimeters when making length measurements.

Use a Tape Measure

1 Measure the distance around a jar. Wrap the tape around the jar.

2 Find the line where the tape begins to wrap over itself.

3 Record the distance around the jar to the nearest centimeter.

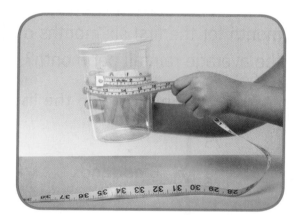

Use a Metric Ruler

1 Measure the length of your shoe. Place the ruler or the meterstick on the floor. Line up the end of the ruler with the heel of your shoe.

2 Notice where the other end of your shoe lines up with the ruler.

3 Look at the scale on the ruler. Record the length of your shoe to the nearest centimeter and to the nearest millimeter.

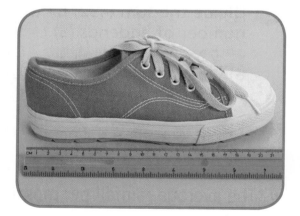

Measuring Volume

A beaker, a measuring cup, and a graduated cylinder are used to measure volume. Volume is the amount of space something takes up. Most of the containers that scientists use to measure volume have a scale marked in milliliters (mL).

Beaker
50 mL

Measuring cup
50 mL

Graduated cylinder
50 mL

Measure the Volume of a Liquid

1. Measure the volume of juice. Pour some juice into a measuring container.

2. Move your head so that your eyes are level with the top of the juice. Read the scale line that is closest to the surface of the juice. If the surface of the juice is curved up on the sides, look at the lowest point of the curve.

3. Read the measurement on the scale. You can estimate the value between two lines on the scale.

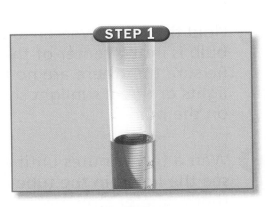

STEP 1

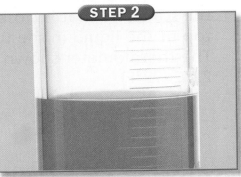

STEP 2

Using a Thermometer

A thermometer is used to measure temperature. When the liquid in the tube of a thermometer gets warmer, it expands and moves farther up the tube. Different scales can be used to measure temperature, but scientists usually use the Celsius scale.

Measure the Temperature of a Liquid

1. Half fill a cup with warm tap water.

2. Hold the thermometer so that the bulb is in the center of the liquid. Be sure that there are no bright lights or direct sunlight shining on the bulb.

3. Wait a few minutes until you see the liquid in the tube of the thermometer stop moving. Read the scale line that is closest to the top of the liquid in the tube. The thermometer shown reads 22°C (72°F).

Using a Balance

A balance is used to measure mass. Mass is the amount of matter in an object. To find the mass of an object, place it in the left pan of the balance. Place standard masses in the right pan.

Measure the Mass of a Ball

1 Check that the empty pans are balanced, or level with each other. When balanced, the pointer on the base should be at the middle mark. If it needs to be adjusted, move the slider on the back of the balance a little to the left or right.

2 Place a ball on the left pan. Then add standard masses, one at a time, to the right pan. When the pointer is at the middle mark again, each pan holds the same amount of matter and has the same mass.

3 Add the numbers marked on the masses in the pan. The total is the mass of the ball in grams.

Making a Chart to Organize Data

A chart can help you keep track of information. When you organize information, or data, it is easier to read, compare, or classify it.

Classifying Animals

Suppose you want to organize this data about animal characteristics. You could base the chart on the two characteristics listed—the number of wings and the number of legs.

1 Give the chart a title that describes the data in it.

2 Name categories, or groups, that describe the data you have collected.

3 Make sure the information is recorded correctly in each column.

Next, you could make another chart to show animal classification based on number of legs only.

My Data

Fleas have no wings. Fleas have six legs.

Snakes have no wings or legs.

A bee has four wings. It has six legs.

Spiders never have wings. They have eight legs.

A dog has no wings. It has four legs.

Birds have two wings and two legs.

A cow has no wings. It has four legs.

A butterfly has four wings. It has six legs.

Animals—Number of Wings and Legs

Animal	Number of Wings	Number of Legs
Flea	0	6
Snake	0	0
Bee	4	6
Spider	0	8
Dog	0	4
Bird	2	2
Butterfly	4	6

Reading a Circle Graph

A circle graph shows a whole divided into parts. You can use a circle graph to compare the parts to each other. You can also use it to compare the parts to the whole.

A Circle Graph of Fuel Use

This circle graph shows fuel use in the United States. The graph has 10 equal parts, or sections. Each section equals $\frac{1}{10}$ of the whole. One whole equals $\frac{10}{10}$.

Oil Of all the fuel used in the United States, 4 out of 10 parts, or $\frac{4}{10}$, is oil.

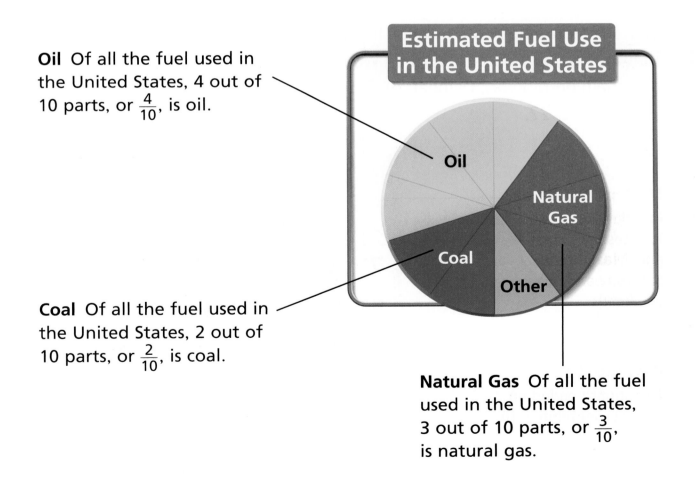

Estimated Fuel Use in the United States

Coal Of all the fuel used in the United States, 2 out of 10 parts, or $\frac{2}{10}$, is coal.

Natural Gas Of all the fuel used in the United States, 3 out of 10 parts, or $\frac{3}{10}$, is natural gas.

Measuring Elapsed Time

A calendar can help you find out how much time has passed, or elapsed, in days or weeks. A clock can help you see how much time has elapsed in hours and minutes. A clock with a second hand or a stopwatch can help you find out how many seconds have elapsed.

Using a Calendar to Find Elapsed Days

This is a calendar for the month of October. October has 31 days. Suppose it is October 22 and you begin an experiment. You need to check the experiment two days from the start date and one week from the start date. That means you would check it on Wednesday, October 24, and again on Monday, October 29. October 29 is 7 days after October 22.

October

Sunday	Monday	Tuesday	Wednesday	Thursday	Friday	Saturday
	1	2	3	4	5	6
7	8	9	10	11	12	13
14	15	16	17	18	19	20
21	22	23	24	25	26	27
28	29	30	31			

Days of the Week
Monday, Tuesday, Wednesday, Thursday, and Friday are weekdays. Saturday and Sunday are weekends.

Last Month
Last month ended on Sunday, September 30.

Next Month
Next month begins on Thursday, November 1.

Using a Clock or a Stopwatch to Find Elapsed Time

You need to time an experiment for 20 minutes.

It is 1:30 P.M.   **Stop at 1:50 P.M.**

You need to time an experiment for 15 seconds. You can use the second hand of a clock or watch.

Start the experiment when the second hand is on number 6.

Stop when 15 seconds have passed and the second hand is on the 9.

You can use a stopwatch to time 15 seconds.

Press the reset button on a stopwatch so that you see 0:00₀₀.

Press the start button. When you see 0:15₀₀, press the stop button.

Measurements

Volume

1 L of sports drink is a little more than 1 qt.

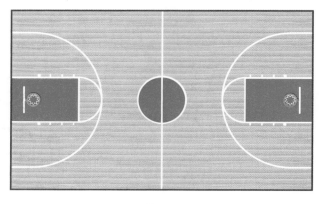

Area

A basketball court covers about 4,700 ft². It covers about 435 m².

Metric Measures

Temperature

- Ice melts at 0 degrees Celsius (°C)
- Water freezes at 0°C
- Water boils at 100°C

Length and Distance

- 1,000 meters (m) = 1 kilometer (km)
- 100 centimeters (cm) = 1 m
- 10 millimeters (mm) = 1 cm

Force

- 1 newton (N) =
  1 kilogram × 1 (meter/second)
  per second

Volume

- 1 cubic meter (m³) = 1 m × 1 m × 1 m
- 1 cubic centimeter (cm³) =
  1 cm × 1 cm × 1 cm
- 1 liter (L) = 1,000 milliliters (mL)
- 1 cm³ = 1 mL

Area

- 1 square kilometer (km²) =
  1 km × 1 km
- 1 hectare = 10,000 m²

Mass

- 1,000 grams (g) = 1 kilogram (kg)
- 1,000 milligrams (mg) = 1 g

Temperature

The temperature at an indoor basketball game might be 27°C, which is 80°F.

Length and Distance

A basketball rim is about 10 ft high, or a little more than 3 m from the floor.

Customary Measures

Temperature

- Ice melts at 32 degrees Fahrenheit (°F)
- Water freezes at 32°F
- Water boils at 212°F

Length and Distance

- 12 inches (in.) = 1 foot (ft)
- 3 ft = 1 yard (yd)
- 5,280 ft = 1 mile (mi)

Weight

- 16 ounces (oz) = 1 pound (lb)
- 2,000 pounds = 1 ton (T)

Volume of Fluids

- 8 fluid ounces (fl oz) = 1 cup (c)
- 2 c = 1 pint (pt)
- 2 pt = 1 quart (qt)
- 4 qt = 1 gallon (gal)

Metric and Customary Rates

km/h = kilometers per hour

m/s = meters per second

mph = miles per hour

Health and Fitness Handbook

Being healthy means that all parts of your body and mind work well together. To keep your body healthy,

- know how to take care of your body systems.
- use safe behaviors when you play.
- choose the right amounts of healthful foods.
- get physical activity every day.
- use behaviors that keep you well.

This handbook will help you learn ways to keep yourself healthy and safe. What will *you* do to stay healthy?

The Nervous System H18
Your nervous system controls your body.

A Nerve Cell H19
Learn how nerve cells carry messages.

Safety in Every Season H20
Find tips to help you stay safe outdoors.

The Exercise Cycle H21
Learn the three parts of a good exercise plan.

Servings for Good Nutrition H22
Find out how many servings to eat of
different kinds of food.

Stop Diseases From Spreading H23
Do you know how to avoid spreading germs? Find out.

The Nervous System

Central Nervous System

Brain The brain is the control center for the body.

Spinal Cord The spinal cord is a bundle of nerves that extends down your back.

- Messages to and from the brain travel through the spinal cord.
- Sometimes the spinal cord sends messages directly to other nerves without sending them to the brain first.

brain

spinal cord

Peripheral Nervous System

Peripheral means "on the outside." Peripheral nerves connect the brain and spinal cord to the rest of the body. There are two kinds of peripheral nerves.

Sensory Nerves These nerves carry messages *to* the central nervous system.

Motor Nerves These nerves carry messages *from* the central nervous system.

The nervous system carries millions of messages every minute. These messages tell you:

- what you see, hear, taste, smell, and touch.
- what you think and how you feel.
- how your body is working.

A Nerve Cell

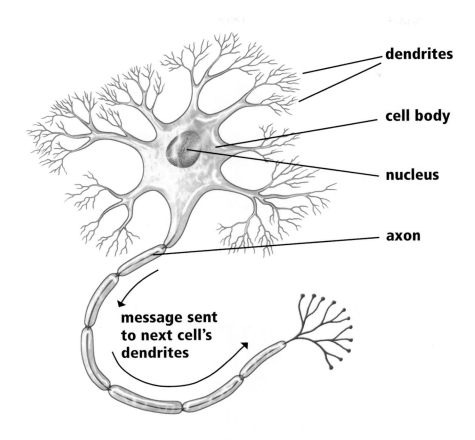

dendrites

cell body

nucleus

axon

message sent to next cell's dendrites

Nerve cells are called *neurons*. They carry messages to and from the brain and spinal cord. You are born with almost all the neurons your body will ever form. Here's an example of how neurons work.

 You touch something hot. Cells in your fingertips send a warning message.

 Dendrites in cells in your sensory nerves pick up the message. They send it to other neurons through their axons.

The message reaches the spinal cord.

 The spinal cord sends messages to motor nerves. The messages cause the muscles in your hand to move away from the hot object.

All of this happens in less time than it takes you to blink!

Safety in Every Season

Being outside in all kinds of weather can be fun! But to be safe, you need to pay attention.

Hot Weather

Protect your skin from the harmful rays of the Sun.

- Always wear sunscreen with a SPF of at least 15.
- Wear sunglasses that protect against UVA and UVB rays.
- Loose-fitting clothes keep you cool and protect your skin. A hat helps, too!
- Drink plenty of water.

Cold Weather

Dress for cold weather in warm layers.

- Wear a hat, gloves or mittens, and socks.
- A waterproof outer layer is a good idea.
- Wear sunscreen. Bright sunlight can reflect from snow and ice.

Water Safety

When swimming:
- always have a buddy.
- know your limits.
- rest often.

Ice Safety

When walking on ice:
- tilt your body forward.
- set your feet down flat.
- take short steps.

Poisonous Plants

If you touch a poisonous plant, rinse the area with rubbing alcohol or water. If a red, itchy rash appears, soak the area with cold water for 10 minutes three times a day. Do not break any blisters.

Stinging Insects

Remove the insect's stinger by scraping it with something stiff, like a credit card. Make a paste of baking soda and water. Apply it to the place where the stinger was. Use a cold pack to help reduce itching and swelling.

The Exercise Cycle

Physical activity is important for good health. It makes your heart, lungs, and muscles strong. It helps you keep a healthful weight, too. It's best to get physical activity every day. When you exercise, include a warm-up, exercise, and a cool-down.

1 **Warm-up** Begin with five minutes of gentle activity. Walking is a good way to warm up your body. Also stretch your muscles gently. This helps prevent injury.

2 **Exercise** Exercise at a steady level for 20 minutes. You should feel your heart beating faster. You should also be breathing hard, but not so hard that you couldn't talk to a friend at the same time.

3 **Cool-down** Exercise at a lower level for about five minutes. Your heart rate and breathing should slow down. Then spend five more minutes stretching your muscles again.

Tips

✔ Drink extra water before, during, and after exercise. This replaces water your body loses when you sweat.

✔ If you are injured or an exercise hurts when you do it, stop right away and tell an adult.

Servings for Good Nutrition

Food gives you energy. It also provides materials your body needs to grow and develop. It's important to eat the right kinds of food in the right amounts and to get physical activity. Together, these will help you maintain a healthful weight.

Food Group	Daily Amount	Examples
Grains	3–6 oz.	bread cereal cooked rice or pasta
Vegetables	2–4 cups	leafy vegetables chopped vegetables, cooked or raw vegetable juice
Fruits	1–2 cups	apple, banana, or orange chopped, cooked, or canned fruit
Milk	2–3 cups	milk or yogurt natural cheese processed cheese
Meat and Beans	5$\frac{1}{2}$ oz.	cooked lean meat, poultry, or fish beans nuts

Stop Diseases From Spreading

Sometimes when you're ill, you have a contagious disease. *Contagious* means that you can spread the illness to others. These diseases are caused by harmful bacteria or viruses that enter the body.

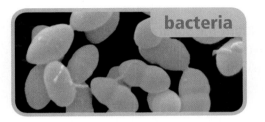

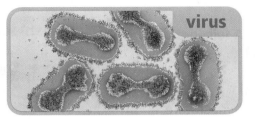

Bacteria cause...

- tetanus
- food poisoning
- strep throat

Viruses cause...

- the common cold
- the flu
- measles
- mumps
- chicken pox

To help stop the spread of these diseases, stay home when you are ill. Also do these things:

- Cover your mouth and nose when you sneeze or cough.
- Throw away tissues after you use them.
- Wash your hands often during the day.
- Keep wounds clean and covered.

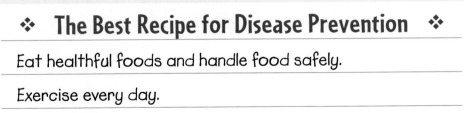

❖ **The Best Recipe for Disease Prevention** ❖

Eat healthful foods and handle food safely.

Exercise every day.

Get plenty of sleep.

Keep your body clean.

Have regular check-ups with your doctor and dentist.

Glossary

A

adaptation (ad ap TAY shuhn) A physical feature or a behavior that helps an organism survive in its habitat. (B60)

adult (uh DUHLT) A fully-grown, mature organism. (A71)

air mass (air mas) A large body of air that has about the same temperature, air pressure, and moisture throughout. (D25)

air pressure (air PRESH uhr) The weight of air as it presses down on Earth's surface. (D8)

analyze data (AN uh lyz DAY tuh) To look for patterns in collected information that lead to making logical inferences, predictions, and hypotheses.

artery (AHR tuh ree) Any blood vessel that carries blood away from the heart to capillaries. (A42)

ask questions (ask KWEHS chuhz) To state orally or in writing questions to find out how or why something happens, which can lead to scientific investigations or research.

atmosphere (AT muh sfihr) The layers of air that surround Earth's surface. (D8)

atom (AT uhm) The smallest particle of matter that has the properties of that matter. (E7)

axis (AK sihs) An imaginary line through the center of an object. (D68)

B

behavior (bih HAYV yur) The way that an organism acts or responds to its environment. (A100)

biodegradable (by oh dih GRAY duh buhl) Able to break down easily in the environment. (C62)

blood (bludh) The substance that carries nutrients and oxygen to every cell in the body. (A36)

C

camouflage (KAM uh flazh) The coloring, marking, or other physical appearance of an animal that helps it blend in with its surroundings. (B62)

capillary (KAP uh layr ee) A tiny blood vessel that connects arteries and veins. (A42)

carnivore (KAHR nuh vawr) An animal that eats only other animals. (B38)

cell (sehl) The basic unit that makes up all living things. (A8)

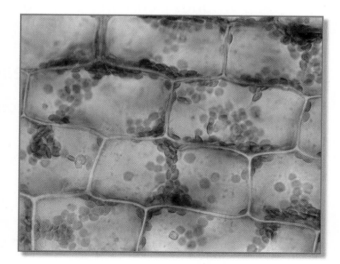

chemical change (KEHM ih kuhl chaynj) A change in matter that produces new kinds of matter with different properties. (E66)

chemical property (KEHM ih kuhl PRAP ur tee) A characteristic of matter that can be observed only when matter is changed into a new kind of matter. (E27)

chemical reaction (KEHM ih kuhl ree AK shuhn) Another term for a chemical change. (E67)

chlorophyll (KLAWR uh fihl) A green material in plants that traps energy from sunlight and gives leaves their green color. (A22)

circulatory system (SUR kyuh luh tawr ee SIHS tuhm) The system that transports oxygen, nutrients, and wastes. (A42)

classify (KLAS uh fy) To sort objects into groups according to their properties or order objects according to a pattern.

climate (KLY muht) The average weather conditions in an area over a long period of time. (D34)

collaborate (kuh LAB uh rayt) To work as a team with others to collect and share data, observations, findings, and ideas.

communicate (kah MYOO nuh kayt) To explain procedures or share information, data, or findings with others through written or spoken words, actions, graphs, charts, tables, diagrams, or sketches.

community (kuh MYOO nih tee) All the organisms that live in the same ecosystem and interact with each other. (B12)

compare (kuhm PAIR) To observe and tell how objects or events are alike or different.

condensation (kahn dehn SAY shuhn) The change of the state of gas to a liquid. (C42, D15)

conduction (kuhn DUHK shuhn) The transfer of thermal energy from particle to particle between two objects that are touching. (F32)

conductors (kuhn DUHK tuhrz) Materials that negatively charged particles can move through easily. (F55)

conservation (kahn sur VAY shuhn) The preserving and wise use of natural resources. (C61)

constellation (KAHN stuh lay shuhn) A group of stars that forms a pattern in the night sky. (D78)

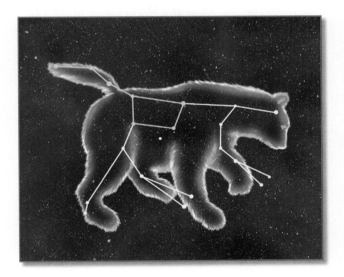

consumer (kuhn SOO mur) An organism that eats other living things to get energy. (B24)

convection (kuhn VEHK shuhn) The transfer of thermal energy by the movement of fluids. (F33)

core (kawr) The innermost layer of Earth. (C7)

crust (kruhst) The outermost layer of Earth. (C6)

D

decay (dih KAY) To break down into simpler materials. (B48)

decomposer (dee kuhm POH zur) An organism that breaks down the remains of dead organisms. (B48)

density (DEHN sih tee) The amount of matter in a given space, or a given volume. (E25)

deposition (dehp uh ZIHSH uhn) The dropping of sediment moved by water, wind, and ice. (C29)

digestive system (dy JEHS tihv SIHS tuhm) One of the body's major organ systems. It processes the food the body takes in. (A33)

dissolve (dih ZAHLV) To mix completely with another substance to form a solution. (E58)

E

ecosystem (EE koh SIHS tuhm) All living and nonliving things that exist and interact in one place. (B6)

egg (ehg) The first stage in the life cycle of most animals. (A70)

electric cell (ih LEHK trihk sehl) A device that turns chemical energy into electrical energy. (F58)

electric charges (ih LEHK trihk CHAHRJ ehs) Tiny particles that carry units of electricity. (F44)

electric circuit (ih LEHK trihk SUR kiht) The pathway that an electric current follows. (F56)

electric current (ih LEHK trihk KUR uhnt) A continuous flow of electric charges. (F54)

electromagnet (ih lehk troh MAG niht) A strong temporary magnet that uses electricity to produce magnetism. (F68)

embryo (EHM bree oh) A plant or animal in the earliest stages of development. (A65)

energy (EHN ur jee) The ability to cause change. (E40)

environment (ehn VY ruhn muhnt) Everything that surrounds and affects a living thing. (A90, B12)

era (IHR uh) A major division of geologic time defined by events that took place during that time. (B79)

erosion (ih ROH zhuhn) The movement of rock material from one place to another. (C28)

esophagus (ih SOHF uh guhs) A muscular tube in the body that pushes food toward the stomach. (A35)

evaporation (ih vap uh RAY shuhn) The change of state from a liquid to a gas. (C42, D15)

experiment (ihks SPEHR uh muhnt) To investigate and collect data that either supports a hypothesis or shows that it is false while controlling variables and changing only one part of an experimental setup at a time.

external stimulus (ihk STUR nuhl STIHM yuh luhs) Anything in an organism's environment that causes it to react. (A94)

extinct (ihk STIHNGKT) No longer living. When the last member of a species has died, the species is extinct. (B70)

F

food chain (food chayn) The path of food energy in an ecosystem as one living thing eats another. (B38)

food web (food wehb) Two or more food chains that overlap. (B40)

force (fawrs) A push that moves an object away or a pull that moves an object nearer. (F90)

fossil (FAHS uhl) The preserved traces and remains of an organism that lived long ago. (B76)

fossil fuel (FAHS uhl FYOO uhl) A fuel that formed from the remains of ancient plants and animals. (C48)

friction (FRIHK shuhn) A force that slows or stops motion between two surfaces that are touching. (F92)

front (fruhnt) The place where two air masses meet. (D26)

G

galaxy (GAL uhk see) A huge system, or group, of stars held together by gravity. (D79)

gas giants (gas JY hunts) The four largest planets in Earth's solar system—Jupiter, Saturn, Uranus, and Neptune—that consist mainly of gases. (D57)

generator (JEHN uh ray tuhr) A devise that uses magnetism to convert energy of motion into electrical energy. (F71)

germinate (JUHR muh nayt) The process in which a seed begins to grow into a new plant. (A65)

gravity (GRAV ih tee) The force that pulls bodies or objects toward other bodies or objects. (D52, F94)

greenhouse effect (GREEN hows ih FEHKT) The process by which heat from the Sun builds up near Earth's surface and is trapped there by the atmosphere. (D10)

habitat (HAB ih tat) The place where an organism lives. (B60)

heart (hahrt) A muscular pump inside the body that pushes the blood through the blood vessels. (A42)

heat (heet) 1. The flow of thermal energy from a warmer area to a cooler area; 2. a measure of how much thermal energy is transferred from one substance to another. (E45, F32)

herbivore (HUR buh vawr) An animal that eats only plants. (B38)

hibernate (HY bur nayt) To go into a deep sleep during which an animal uses very little energy and usually does not need to eat. (B64)

humus (HYOO muhs) A material made up of decayed plant and animal matter. (C52)

hypothesize (hy PAHTH uh syz) To make an educated guess about why something happens.

igneous rock (IHG nee uhs rahk) The type of rock that is formed when melted rock from inside Earth cools and hardens. (C8)

inclined plane (ihn KLYND playn) A simple machine made up of a slanted surface. (F100)

infer (ihn FUR) To use facts and data you know and observations you have made to draw a conclusion about a specific event based on observations and data. To construct a reasonable explanation.

inherit (ihn HEHR iht) To receive traits from parents. (A79)

inherited behavior (ihn HEHR iht uhd bih HAYV yur) A behavior that an organism is born with and does not need to learn. (A100)

instinct (IHN stihngkt) A complex pattern of behavior that organisms of the same type are born with. (A101)

insulators (IHN suh lay tuhrz) Materials that electric charges do not flow through easily. (F55)

internal stimulus (ihn TUR nuhl STIHM yuh luhs) Anything within an organism that causes it to react. (A94)

kinetic energy (kuh NEHT ihk EHN ur jee) The energy that an object has because it is moving. (F7)

L

large intestine (lahrj ihn TEHS tihn) The organ where water and minerals from food are removed and absorbed into the blood. (A36)

larva (LAHR vuh) The wormlike form that hatches from an egg. The second stage of an organism that goes through complete metamorphosis. (A71)

lava (LAH vuh) Molten rock that reaches Earth's surface, such as when a volcano erupts. (C16)

leaf (leef) The part of a plant that uses sunlight and air to help the plant make food. (A18)

learned behavior (lurnd bih HAYV yur) A behavior that is taught or learned from experience. (A102)

lever (LEHV ur) A simple machine made up of a stiff bar that moves freely around a fixed point. (F102)

life cycle (lyf SY kuhl) A series of stages that occur during the lifetimes of all organisms. (A64)

life process (lyf PRAHS ehs) A function that an organism performs to stay alive and produce more of its own kind. (A6)

life span (lyf span) The length of time it takes for an individual organism to complete its life cycle. (A66)

light (lyt) A form of energy that travels in waves and can be seen when it interacts with matter. (F12)

lunar eclipse (LOO nur ih KLIHPS) An event in which the Moon passes into Earth's shadow. (D71)

M

magma (MAG muh) Molten rock beneath Earth's surface. (C16)

magnet (MAG niht) An object that attracts certain metals, mainly iron. (F62)

magnetic field (MAG neht ihk feeld) The space in which the force of a magnet can act. (F63)

magnetic poles (mag NEHT ihk pohlz) The two areas on a magnet with the greatest magnetic force. (F63)

mantle (MAN tl) A thick layer of rock between Earth's crust and core. (C7)

mass (mas) The amount of matter in an object. (E16)

matter (MAT ur) Anything that has mass and takes up space. (E6)

measure (MEHZH uhr) To use a variety of measuring instruments and tools to find the length, distance, volume, mass, or temperature using appropriate units of measurement.

metamorphic rock (meht uh MAWR fihk rahk) New rock that forms when existing rocks are changed by heat, pressure, or chemicals. (C9)

metamorphosis (meht uh MAWR fuh sihs) The process in which some organisms change form in different stages of their life cycles. (A71)

metric system (MEHT rihk SIHS tuhm) A system of measurement based on multiples of 10. (E14)

microorganism (my kroh AWR guh nihz uhm) A tiny living thing that can only be seen with a microscope. (B49)

migrate (MY grayt) To move to another region when seasons change and food supplies become scarce. (B70)

mimicry (MIHM ih kree) An adaptation that allows an animal to protect itself by looking like another kind of animal or like a plant. (B63)

mineral (MIHN ur uhl) A solid, nonliving material of specific chemical makeup. (C6)

mixture (MIHKS chur) Matter made up of two or more substances or materials that are physically combined. (E54)

molecule (MAHL ih kyool) A single particle of matter made up of two or more atoms joined together. (E7)

motion (MOH shuhn) A change in an object's position as compared to objects around it. (F82)

motor (MOH tur) A device that changes electrical energy into energy of motion. (F70)

muscular system (MUHS kyuh luhr SIHS tuhm) A system made up of muscles, tissues that make body parts move. (A54)

natural resource (NACH ur uhl REE sawrs) A material on Earth that is useful to people. (C40)

niche (nihch) The role a plant or animal plays in its habitat. (B60)

nonrenewable resource (nahn rih NOO uh buhl REE sawrs) A natural resource that cannot be replaced once it is used up or that takes thousands of years to be replaced. (C40)

nymph (nihmf) The second stage of an insect as it goes through incomplete metamorphosis. (A71)

observe (UHB zuhrv) To use the senses and tools to gather or collect information and determine the properties of objects or events.

omnivore (AHM nuh vawr) An animal that eats both plants and animals. (B38)

orbit (AWR biht) The path that Earth and eight other planets make as they move around the Sun. (D50)

organ (AWR guhn) A special part of an organism's body that performs a specific function. (A11)

organism (AWR guh nihz uhm) Any living thing that can carry out life processes on its own. (A10)

organic matter (awr GAN ihk MAT ur) The remains of plants and animals. (B6)

organ system (AWR guhn SIHS tuhm) A group of organs that work together to carry out life processes. (A12)

paleontologist (pay lee ahn TAHL uh jihst) A scientist who studies fossils. (B77)

parallel circuit (PAR uh lehl SUR kiht) A circuit in which the parts are connected so that the electric current passes along more than one pathway. (F57)

phases of the Moon (FAYZ ihz uhv thuh moon) Changes in the amount of the sunlit half of the Moon that can be seen from Earth. (D71)

photosynthesis (foh toh SIHN thih sihs) The process plants use to make food. (B36, A22)

physical change (FIHZ ih kuhl chaynj) A change in the size, shape, or state of matter that does not change it into a new kind of matter. (E38)

physical property (FIHZ ih kuhl PRAP ur tee) A characteristic of matter that can be measured or observed without changing matter into something new. (E10)

planet (PLAN iht) A large body of rock or gas that does not produce its own light and orbits around a star. (D50)

polar climate (POH lur KLY muht) Places with polar climate have very cold temperatures throughout the year, and are located around the North Pole and the South Pole. (D35)

pollinator (PAHL uh nay tur) An animal, such as an insect or bird, that helps plants make seeds by moving pollen from one part of the plant to another. (B26)

pollutant (puh LOOT uhnt) Any harmful material added to the air, the water, and the soil. (C60)

pollution (puh LOO shuhn) The addition of harmful materials to the air, the water, and the soil. (C51)

population (pahp yuh LAY shun) All the organisms of the same kind that live in an ecosystem. (B12)

position (puh ZIHSH uhn) An object's location, or place. (F82)

potential energy (puh TEHN shuhl EHN ur jee) The energy that is stored in an object. (F7)

prairie (PRAIR ee) A grassy land area with few or no trees. (B14)

precipitation (prih sihp ih TAY shuhn) Any form of water that falls from clouds to Earth's surface. (C42, D16)

predator (PREHD uh tawr) An animal that hunts other animals for food. (B37)

predict (prih DIHKT) To state what you think will happen based on past experience, observations, patterns, and cause-and-effect relationships.

prey (pray) An animal that is hunted for food by a predator. (B37)

producer (pruh DOO sur) Any organism that makes its own food. (B24)

product (PRAHD uhkt) The newly formed matter in a chemical reaction. (E67)

pulley (PUL ee) A simple machine made up of a rope fitted around the rim of a fixed wheel. (F103)

radiation (ray dee AY shuhn) The transfer of energy by waves. (F34)

rainforest (RAYN fawr ihst) An area with a great deal of rainfall. Most rainforests are warm all year, and there is a lot of sunlight. (B14)

reactant (ree AK tuhnt) The matter that you start with in a chemical reaction. (E67)

record data (rih KAWRD DAY tuh) To write (in tables, charts, journals), draw, audio record, video record, or photograph, to show observations.

recycling (ree SY kuhl ihng) The process of breaking down materials into a different form that is used again. (B48)

reflection (rih FLEHK shuhn) What occurs when light waves bounce off a surface. (F14)

refraction (rih FRAK shuhn) What occurs when light waves bend as they pass from one material to another. (F14)

renewable resource (rih NOO uh buhl REE sawrs) A natural resource that can be replaced or can replace or renew itself. (C40)

reproduce (ree pruh DOOS) When organisms make more organisms of their own kind. (A6)

reproduction (ree pruh DUHK shun) The process of making more of one's own kind. (B26)

research (rih SURCH) To learn more about a subject by looking in books, newspapers, magazines, CD-ROMs, searching the Internet, or asking science experts.

respiratory system (REHS puhr uh tawr ee SIHS tuhm) A group of organs that work together to take air into the body and push it back out. (A40)

response (rih SPAHNS) A reaction to a stimulus. (A91)

revolution (rehv uh LOO shuhn) The movement in a path around an object, as when the Earth travels around the Sun; one complete trip around the Sun. (D72)

rock (rahk) A solid material that is made up of one or more minerals. (C6)

rock cycle (rahk SY kuhl) The continuous series of changes that rocks go through. (C10)

root (root) The part of a plant that takes in water and nutrients from the ground. (A18)

rotation (roh TAY shuhn) The turning of a planet on its axis. (D68)

scavenger (SKAV uhn jur) An animal that feeds on the remains of dead animals. (B46)

screw (skroo) A simple machine made up of an inclined plane wrapped around a column. (F101)

sediment (SEHD uh muhnt) Sand, particles of rock, bits of soil, and the remains of once-living things. (C8)

sedimentary rock (sehd uh MEHN tuh ree rahk) A type of rock that forms when sediment becomes pressed together and hardens. (C8)

seed (seed) An undeveloped plant sealed in a protective coating. (A19)

seed dispersal (seed dih SPUR suhl) The scattering or carrying away of seeds from the plant that produced them. (B26)

series circuit (SIHR eez SUR kiht) A circuit in which the parts are connected so that the electric current passes through each part along a single pathway. (F57)

simple machine (SIHM puhl muh SHEEN) A device that changes a force. (F100)

skeletal system (SKEHL ih tuhl SIHS tuhm) The bones that give the body shape and support, protect the organs inside the body, and work with the muscles to move the body. (A52)

small intestine (smawl ihn TEHS tihn) The long, coiled organ where most digestion takes place. (A36)

soil (soyl) The loose material that covers much of Earth's surface. (B6)

soil profile (soyl PROH fyl) A lengthwise cross section of soil that shows the different layers. (C52)

solar system (SOH lur SIHS tuhm) A system made up of the Sun, nine planets, and smaller bodies that orbit the Sun. (D50)

solution (suh LOO shuhn) A mixture in which the particles of one kind of matter are mixed evenly with the particles of other kinds of matter. (E58)

sound (sownd) A form of energy that is produced by vibrations and can be heard. (F20)

species (SPEE sheez) A group of organisms that produces organisms of the same kind. (B70)

speed (speed) A measure of the distance an object travels in a certain amount of time. (F84)

star (stahr) A huge ball of very hot gases that gives off light, heat, and other kinds of energy. (D76)

states of matter (stayts uhv MAT ur) The three forms that matter usually takes: solid, liquid, and gas. (E8)

static electricity (STAT ihk ih lehk TRIHS ih tee) An electric charge that builds up on a material. (F46)

stem (stehm) The part of the plant that carries food, water and nutrients to and from the roots and leaves. (A18)

stimulus (STIHM yuh luhs) Anything that causes a living thing to react. (A91)

stomach (STUHM uhk) A muscular organ in the body that mixes and stores food and turns in into a soupy mix. (A35)

temperate climate (TEHM pur iht KLY muht) Places with temperate climate usually have warm, dry summers and cold, wet winters. (D35)

temperate zone (TEHM pur iht zohn) An area of Earth where the temperature rarely gets very hot or very cold. The temperate zones are located between the tropical zone and the polar zones. (B15)

temperature (TEHM pur uh chur)
1. A measure of how hot or cold matter is;
2. the average kinetic energy of the particles of a substance. (E46, F31)

thermal energy (THUR muhl EHN ur jee) The total kinetic energy of tiny moving particles of matter. (E44, F30)

tissue (TIHSH oo) A group of similar cells that work together. (A12)

topsoil (TAHP soyl) The upper layer of soil that contains minerals and humus. (C52)

trait (trayt) A feature or characteristic of a living thing. (A79)

tropical climate (TRAHP ih kuhl KLY miht) Places with tropical climate are hot and rainy for most of or all of the year. (D35)

universe (YOO nuh vurs) The system made up of all the matter and energy there is, including the galaxies, and their stars, planets, and moons. (D79)

use models (yooz MAHD lz) To use sketches, diagrams or other physical representation of an object, process, or idea to better understand or describe how it works.

use numbers (yooz NUHM burz) To use numerical data to count, measure, estimate, order, and record data to compare objects and events.

use variables (yooz VAIR ee uh buhlz) To keep all conditions in an experiment the same except for the variable, or the condition that is being tested in the experiment.

vein (vayn) Any blood vessel that carries blood back to the heart. (A42)

velocity (vuh LAHS ih tee) A measure of speed in a certain direction. (F86)

vibration (vy BRAY shuhn) A back-and-forth movement of matter. (F20)

volume (VAHL yoom) 1. The amount of space that matter takes up; 2. The loudness of a sound. (E17, F22)

water cycle (WAH tur SY kuhl) The movement of water into the air as water vapor and back to Earth's surface as precipitation. (D16)

weather (WEHTH ur) The conditions of the atmosphere at a certain place and time. (D9)

weathering (WEHTH ur ihng) The slow wearing away of rock into smaller pieces. (C26)

wedge (wehj) A simple machine made up of two inclined planes. (F101)

weight (wayt) The measure of the pull of gravity on an object. (E18)

wheel and axle (hweel and AK suhl) A simple machine made up of two cylinders that turn on the same axis. (F102)

Index

A

Acid, A35
Acid rain, C27
Adaptations, B60–B64
Adirondack Mountains, C30
Air
  composition of, D6–D7
  in forest ecosystem, B7
  and mixtures, E57
  as natural resource, C40
Air masses, D25–D26, D37
Air pollution, C51
Air pressure, D8, D22–D23
Air resistance, F92
Air sacs, A40, A41
Airplanes, F106–F107
Algae, A10
Alligators, A70, A72
Aloe vera, C41
Alps, mountains, D37
Altitude, D37
Amphibians, A70
Amplitude, F12, F22
Anemometer, D23
Angelfish, A52
Animals
  adaptations of, B60–B64
  behavior of, A100–A103,
    B64
  bones of, A52
  cells of, A8–A9
  life cycle of, A70–A72
  life span of, A72
  and reaction to
    surroundings,
    A91–A94
  as renewable resources,
    C41
  response to stimuli,
    A90–A94

Antacids, E69
Antarctica, D30–D31, D38
Anthracite, coal, C49
Ants, B22
Arctic fox, B62
Armstrong, Neil, D65
Arteries, A42–A43
Aspirin, C41
Astrolabe, D64
Astronomers, D64
Aswan Dam, B69
Atmosphere, D6–D10, D38
Atoms
  changes in, E67, E69, E71
  and molecules, E7–E9
Atriums, heart, A44
Auroras, D82
Axis
  of Earth, D68, D72
  of Moon, D71
  of planets, D72
Aye aye, B61

B

Bacteria, A10, B48, B49
Baking soda, E65, E69
Balance scale, E16
Ball bearings, F93
Balloons
  changes in, E1, E39,
    E46, E80
  and static electricity, F45
Barometer, D23
Bats, A1, A92, A112, B77
Battery, E68, F57, F58
Bean plants, A66
Bears, A72, A78, A102
Beavers, B13
Bedrock, C52
Bees, A92
Beetles, A24–A25, A71,
  B46, B52–B53
Bell, Alexander Graham,
  F26–F27
Bengal tigers, B62

Big Dipper, D78
Biodegradable materials,
  C62, E30–E31
Birds, A70, A72, A79
Bison, B70
Bituminous coal, C49
Blizzards, D28
Blood, A36, A40–A43
Blood circulation, A46–A49
Blood clots, A43
Blood vessels, A42–A43
Blue whale, F36–F37
Boiling, E48, E49
Bones, A52–A53
Breastbone, A53
Breathing, A40, A41
Bubbles, E56
Bumble bees, B63
Burning, E27, E28, E66, E68
Butterflies, B63

C

Cactuses, A21
Camouflage, B62
Cancer drug, E20–E21
Capillaries, A42–A43
Carbohydrates, A33–A34,
  A36
Carbon, B79
Carbon dioxide, A22,
  A40–A41, B36, D7
Cardiac muscle, A54
Caribou, B70
Carnivores, B38–B39,
  B47, B48
Carrion beetles, A24, B46
Carson, Rachel, B42–B43
Cartilage, A53
Cassini spacecraft, D59
Cell membrane, A8–A9
Cell wall, A8
Cells, A8–A9
Celsius scale, E46–E47
Cenozoic Era, B79
Centimeters, E14–E15, E17

Chemical bonds, E69, E70
Chemical changes, E66–E71
Chemical combination, E71
Chemical compound, E71
Chemical energy, F8
Chemical properties, E27–E28
Chemical reaction, E67–E69
Chimpanzees, A102
Chlorophyll, A8, A22
Chloroplasts, A8, A22
Chromosomes, A8–A9
Circuit box, F58
Circuit breaker, F58
Circuit pathways, F57
Circulatory system, A42–A44, A46–A49
Cirrus clouds, D17
Clay soil, C53
Climate, D34–D38
Climate zones, D35
Clouds, C42, D16–D17, F48–F51
Clown fish, B23
Coal,
  coke from, C49
  formation of, C49
  as fossil fuel, C48
Color
  and light, F15–F16
  of matter, E6, E24, E50
Comets, D62
Community, B12
Compass, F64
Compost, B50
Condensation
  and clouds, D16–D17
  as physical change, E48, E49
  and water cycle, D16–D17, D49
  and water vapor, C39, C42
Conduction, F32
Conductors, F55, F57, F70
Conservation, B72–B73, C60–C63

Constellations, D78
Consumers, B24–B25, B36, B37, B46
Continents, C6
Convection, F33
Cooking, E28, E66–E67, F32
Copper, E70
Coral reef ecosystem, B1, B16, B88
Core, of Earth, C7
Crabs, A82–A83, B25
Crafty Canines, B19
Crayfish, A92
Crickets, A92
Crocodile, B23
Crust, of Earth, C6, C8–C9, C15
Crystals, C8
Cubic centimeters, E17
Cumulonimbus clouds, D17
Cumulus clouds, D17
Cylinders, E17
Cytoplasm, A8–A9, A11

Day and night, D68–D69
Decay, B48–B50
Decibels, F36–F37
Decomposers, B48–B50
Deer, B13, B39, B62
Deinotherium, fossil, B78
Density, E25, E50, E55
Deposition, C29
  see also Erosion
Desert, D37
Desert ecosystem, B8, B61
Diaphragm, A40–A41
Diatoms, A10
Digestion, A34–A36
Digestive system, A12, A32–A36
Dinosaurs, B76, B79
Direction, and motion, F86
Disease, A10, B48
Distance, measuring, F84–F85

Dogs, A94, A103
Dolphins, A92, B60
Douglas, Marjory Stoneman, B72
Ducks, A6, B60
Dung beetles, B52–B53

E. coli, A10
Eagles, B73
Eardrum, F24
Ears, A90, F24
Earth
  atmosphere of, D6–D10, D38
  axis of, D68, D72
  core of, C7
  crust of, C6–C7, C8–C9, C15
  diameter of, D48, D51, D57
  gravity of, D52
  layers of, C6–C7
  as magnet, F64
  mantle of, C7, C16
  mass of, D51, D57
  and Moon, D57, D70–D71
  orbit of, D50–D51, D68–D69
  revolution of, D72
  rotation of, D68–D69, D72, D78
  and Sun, D48–D49, D56
  surface of, C26–C30, D51
  warming of, D38, D48–D49
  water on, C42–C43, D14
Earth Day, B73
Earthquakes, C14–C15, C18
Echolocation, A92, A112
Eclipse, of Moon, D71
Ecosystems
  and living things, B12–B16

and nonliving things,
B6–B8
relationships in, B24–B25
types of, B7–B8,
B12–B16, B37–B39
see also Environment

Eggs
of amphibians, A70
of animals, A70
of birds, A70, A72
of fish, A70
of insects, A70, A71
and life cycle, A70–A71
of reptiles, A70
Egyptian plover, B23
El Niño, D36
Electric cell, F58
Electric charges, F44–F46,
F54–F55
Electric circuit, F56–F58
Electric cord, F54–F55
Electric current, F54–F58,
F71
Electric eel, F74–F75
Electric fuses, F58
Electric motor, F70
Electric outlet, F54
Electric switch, F52, F56
Electric wires, F71
Electrical appliances,
F54–F55, F58, F72
Electrical energy, F8
Electrician, F105
Electricity
cost of, F72
from fossil fuels,
C48–C51
generating, F58, F71
and magnetism, F68–F71
saving, F72
Electromagnets, F68–F70
Elephants, A72, B78
Elion, Gertrude Belle,
E20–E21
Embryo, A65, A70
Endurance, D30–D31

Energy
changes in, E40, E44–E45,
E66–E69, F7–F8
from food, B34–B40
forms of, E46–E49, F6–F8,
F12–F13, F19–F21,
F30–F33
from fossil fuels, C48–C51
from Sun, B36, C51,
D48–D49, D76
Energy transformation, F8
Environment
changes in, B68–B69
for living things, B12
protecting, C61
reacting to, A90–A94
see also Ecosystems
Environmental technicians,
D81
Enzymes, A34, A35
Equator, D25, D35, D36
Erosion, C28–C29. *See also*
Weathering *and*
Deposition.
Eruptive prominence,
D82–D83
Esophagus, A35
Evaporation, C42, D15–D16,
D49, E49
Exhaling, A40, A41
Exoskeleton, A52
External stimulus, A90, A94
Extinction, B70, B78
Eyes, A90

Fahrenheit scale, E46–E47
Fats, as nutrients, A33, A36
Faults, C14–C16, C30
Femur, bone, A53
Fertilizers, C44
Fiber optics, F27
Fibrous root system, A20
Fibula, bone, A53
Fir trees, A66

Fire investigator, E73
Fires, C18, E66
"First Snow," E62–E63
Fish
eggs of, A70
gills of, A40
instincts of, A101
and interdependence,
B23, B82
skeletal system of, A52
in tropical climate, D34
Five senses, A90–A91
Flight, E1, E46, E80,
F106–F107
Florida Everglades, B15,
B72
Flowers, A19, A24–A25,
A64–A65, B26
Fog, E57
Food
changes in, E66–E68
cooking, E28, E66–E67,
F32
digesting, A32–A36
see also Nutrients
Food chains, B38–B40
Food science technician,
E73
Food webs, B40
Forces, and motion,
F90–F94
Forest destruction, C61
Forest ecosystem, B6–B7,
B12–B13
Forest fires, C18
Forest food chain, B38–B39
Fossil fuels, C48–C51
Fossil tree fern, B76
Fossils, B76–B79, D38
Fox, B37, B40
Franklin, Benjamin, F48–F51
Freezing, E48–E49
Frequency, F22–F23
Friction, F86, F90–F94
Frogs, A80, B63

Fuel oil, C50
Fulgurites, E74–E75
Fungi, B48, B49, B68

Galaxies, D79
Galilei, Galileo, D64
Galle, Johann, D65
Garbage, B50, C60–C61
Gas giants, D57–D61
Gases
  in atmosphere, D6–D10
  changes in, E48–E49
  mixtures of, E56
  particles of, E48–E49
  properties of, E8–E10
  water vapor, D14, E8–E9
Generator, F71
Geologic time scale, B79
Germination, A65, A66
Gills, A40
Giraffes, E14, E15
Glaciers, C28–C29
Golden Hoard, The,
  E62–E63
Goldenrod spider, B83
Goosefish, B82
Grams, E16
Grand Canyon, C20–C23
Grasshoppers, B40
Gravity
  of Earth, D52
  and friction, F86, F90–F94
  of Moon, D52
  and weight, D52, E18
Great horned owl, B38–B39
Green homes, C56–C57
Greenhouse effect, D10
Grizzly bear, A72
Grosbeak weaver birds,
  A101
Groundwater, D16
Group hunting, B64

Habitats, B60–B61
  See also Ecosystems;
  Environment
Hail, D18
Hearing, A90, A92, F24
Heart, A42, A44, A54
Heat
  from Sun, D10, D24, F13
  from thermal energy,
    E45, F30–F32
Helios, F106–F107
Herbivores, B38, B39
Hermit crabs, B25
Herschel, William, D60, D64
Hibernation, A101, B64
Himalayas, mountains, C30
Hitchings, Dr. George,
  E20–E21
Hooke, Robert, A14–A15
Hot-air balloon, E1, E46,
  E80
Human body
  circulatory system,
    A42–A44, A46–A49
  digestive system,
    A32–A36
  muscular system, A54
  respiratory system,
    A40–A41, A46–A49
  skeletal system, A52–A53
Humans
  inheriting traits, A79
  life span of, A72
  traits in, A79
Humerus, bone, A53
Humidity, D22, D25
Humpback whales, B64
Humus, C52, C53
Hurricanes, D22, D28
Hydroelectric power, C51
Hypatia, D64

Ice
  freezing, D14
  melting, D15, E39–E40,
    E48–E50
  as solid, E8–E9
  and weathering, C27
Igneous rock, C8–C10
In-line skates, F96–F97
Inclined plane, F100
Infrared camera, E47
Inhaling, A40, A41
Inheriting behavior, A100
Inheriting traits, A78–A80
Insects
  eggs of, A70, A71
  inheriting traits, A79
  instincts of, A101
  as pollinators, B26
Instinct, A101
Insulators, F55
Internal stimulus, A94
Intestines, A36
Iron, E44–E45, E50
Iron filings, E54, F63

Jackrabbit, B61
Jellies, A11
Joints, A53
Jupiter, D57, D58, D72

Kapok tree, B24
Kilograms, E16
Kilometers, E14–E15
Kinetic energy, F6–F8,
  F30–F31
Kingfisher, A94

Landfills, C60
Landforms, C15
Landscaper, B81
Landslides, C18
Large intestine, A36
Larva, A71
Latitude, D36
Lava, C16–C17, C32–C33
Leaf-cutter ants, B68
Leafy sea dragon, B63
Learned behavior,
   A102–A103
Leaves
   and photosynthesis, A22,
      B36, D49
   role of, A18–A20, A22
   types of, A20
Lemur, A79
Lever, F102
Licensed practical nurse,
   A105
Life cycles
   of animals, A70–A72
   of plants, A64–A65
Life processes, A6–A7,
   A16–A22
Life span
   of animals, A72
   of plants, A66
Ligaments, A53
Light
   absorption of, F15
   behavior of, F12–F16
   and color, F15–F16
   in forest ecosystem, B7
   properties of, F12–F13
   reflection of, D50,
      D70–D71, F14
   speed of, F85
   from Sun, D76, F13
Light bulbs, F56, F57
Light energy, F8, F12–F13

Light switch, F56
Light waves, F12–F15,
   F26–F27
Lightning, D40–D41,
   E74–E75, F48–F51
Lightning fossils, E74–E75
Lignite, coal, C49
Liquids
   changes in, E48–E49
   measuring, E17
   mixtures of, E56
   particles of, E44–E45,
      E48–E49
   properties of, E8–E10
   volume of, E17
Liters, E17
Liver, A36
Living things
   adaptations of, B60–B64
   characteristics of, A6–A12,
      A78–A80
   community of, B12
   and ecosystems, B12–B16
   inheriting traits, A78–A80
   and interdependence,
      B22–B23
   and reproduction, A6–A7,
      A64–A65, A70–A72,
      B26
   roles of, B22–B26
   see also Organisms
Lizards, A12, A72
Loam, C53
Lunar eclipse, D71
Lungs, A40–A41

Macaws, B24
Magma, C16–C17
Magnetic compass, F64
Magnetic field, F63, F64
Magnetic poles, F63, F64,
   F70
Magnetism, F62, F68–F71

Magnets, F62–F63
Mammals, A72. *See also*
   Animals
Manatees, B28–B29
Mantle, of Earth, C7, C16
Many-celled organisms,
   A11
Maple trees, A66
Marabou storks, B47
Mars, D56, D57, D65, D72
Mars rovers, D65
Mass, E14–E16, E50
Materials
   biodegradable materials,
      C62, E30–E31
   recycling materials, C58,
      C62–C63
   reusing materials,
      C62–C63
Matter
   chemical changes in,
      E66–E71
   classifying, E24–E25
   and energy, E40, E44–E45
   examples of, E6, E26
   makeup of, E6–E7
   mass of, E16
   measuring, E14–E19
   observing, E6–E7
   particles of, E7–E8,
      E44–E49
   physical changes in, E10,
      E38–E40, E44–E49,
      E70–E71
   properties of, E6–E8,
      E24–E27, E50
   states of, E8, E10, E48–E49
   volume of, E17
Mealworms, A71
Mechanical energy, F8
Melting, D15, E39–E40,
   E48–E50, E74–E75
Mercury, D56, D57, D72
Merlin, Joseph, F96
Mesosphere, D9

Index

Mesozoic Era, B79
Metals, E27–E28, E50, E68, E70
Metamorphic rock, C9–C10
Metamorphosis, A71
Meteorologists, D27, D28, D81
Meters, E14–E15
Metric ruler, E14–E15
Metric system, E14–E15
Metric units, E15, E17
Mexican bean beetle, A71
Micrographia, A14–A15
Microorganisms, B49
Microscopes, A14, E6–E7
Midnight Fox, The, B18
Migration, A101, B70
Milky Way Galaxy, D79
Milliliters, E17
Mimicry, B63
Minerals
    digestion of, A36
    as nutrients, A33
    rocks, C6, C8
    in soil, C52
Mist, D15
Mites, C66–C67
Mitochondria, A8–A9
Mixtures, E54–E60, E71
Moeritherium, B78
Mold, B48
Molecules
    and atoms, E7–E9
    changes in, E67, E69, E71
Moles, A91
Molten rock, C10, C16
Monkeys, A103, B25
Moon
    axis of, D71
    diameter of, D51
    and Earth, D57, D68–D71
    eclipse of, D71
    gravity of, D52
    and light, D50, D70–D71
    mass of, D51
    orbit of, D70–D71

phases of, D70–D71
    rotation of, D71
    surface of, D51
    walking on, D65
Moths, A92
Motion, F82–F85, F90–F94
Motors, F70
Mount Paricutín, C30
Mount St. Helens, C16–C18
Mountain lion, A72
Mountains, C15–C17, C30, D37
Mouse, A72
Mudslides, C18
Muir, John, B72, B73
Muscles, A54, A56–A57
Muscular system, A54
Mushrooms, B48
Musical instruments, F21, F22
Musk ox, B61

National Park Service, B72
Natural gas, C50
Natural resources, C48–C54, C60–C63
Nectar, B26
Neptune, D57, D61, D65, D72
Niche, B60
Night vision goggles, A96–A97
Nile River, B69
Nitrogen, D6–D7
Nonliving things, B6–B8
Nonrenewable resources, C40, C48–C54
North Pole, D25, F64
Nose, A41, A90
Nucleus, A8–A9
Nutrients
    in blood, A36, A42–A43
    in food, A33

energy from, A32
    and life processes, A6–A7
    in soil, B48–B50, C44, C52
    types of, A33
    see also Food
Nymph, A71

Oceans
    currents of, D36
    and deposition, C29
    ecosystems in, B16
    as habitat, B60
    interdependence in, B23
    warming of, D24, D36, D48
    and water cycle, D16
    and weathering, C26
Offspring, A71, A78–A80
Oil, C50–C51
Olsen, Brennan, F96
Olsen, Scott, F96
Omnivores, B38, B39, B47
Opossum, B60
Opportunity, Mars rover, D65
Orb spiders, A101
Orbit, D50–D51, D68–D71
Orca whale, A102
Orchard Book of Greek Myths, The, A74
Organ system,
    circulatory system, A42–A44, A46–A49
    digestive system, A32–A36
    muscular system, A54
    organization of, A11–A12
    respiratory system, A40–A41, A46–A49
    skeletal system, A52–A53
Organic matter, B6
Organisms
    adaptations of, B60–B64

inheriting traits, A78–A80
response to stimuli, A90–A94
types of, A10–A12
see also Living things
Otters, A93, A102
Owl butterfly, B63
Owls, B38–B40
Oxygen
in blood, A46–A49
need for, D6–D7
from plants, A10, A22

Pacific yew trees, A66
Paleontologist, B77–B79
Paleozoic Era, B79
Palm tree, A79
Pancreas, A36
Pandas, B66
Parallel circuit, F57–F58
Park ranger, B81
Parkes Radio Telescope, D65
Particles
and chemical changes, E67, E70
of matter, E7–E8, E44–E49
movement of, E44–E49, F30–F33
observing, E6–E7
and physical changes, E44–E49
Passenger pigeons, B70
Pathologist, A105
Peat, C49
Peccaries, B47
Pelvis, bone, A53
Petals, A64, A65
Phiomia, B78
Photosynthesis, A22, B36, B38, D49

Physical changes, of matter, E10, E38–E40, E44–E50, E70–E71
Physical combination, E71
Physical properties, of matter, E10, E24–E26
Pigeons, Passenger, B70
Pistil, A64, A65
Pitch, F23
Planets, D50–D51, D56–D62, D72
Plant cells, A8
Plants
adaptation of, B60–B61
classifying, A20–A21
energy from, B37–B38
in food chain, B38–B39, B40
inheriting traits, A79–A80
life cycle of, A64–A65
life span of, A66
nutrients for, C44
parts of, A18–A21
as producers, B24
as renewable resources, C41
reproduction of, A64–A65, B26
response to stimuli, A91, A94
and sunlight, D49
see also Trees
Platelets, A43
Plimpton, James, F96
Pluto, D57, D62, D72
Poison dart frog, B63
Polar air masses, D25
Polar bears, A78
Polar climate, D35
Polar ecosystem, B8
Poles, D25, D38, F63–F64, F70
Pollen, A64–A65, B26
Pollination, A64–A65, B26
Pollinators, B26

Pollutants, C60
Pollution, C51, C60
Pond ecosystem, B37, B39
Pond food chain, B39
Ponderosa pine trees, A66
Populations, B12
Position, and motion, F82–F83
Potential energy, F6–F8
Powell, John Wesley, C20–C23
Powell Expedition, C20–C23
Prairie ecosystem, B14
Praying mantis, B83
Precipitation, C42, D16, D18, D23
Predators, B37, B39, B47, B62–B64
Prey, B37, B39, B46–B47, B63–B64
Prism, F16
Producers, B24, B37, B38
Protection, B22, B25
Proteins, A32–A33, A35–A36
Pterosaur, B77
Pull, F90–F91, F94
Pulley, F103
Pulse, A44
Pupa, A71
Push, F90–F91
Pygmy seahorse, B83

Rabbits, A91, B25, B37, B64
Raccoons, A102, B39, B40
Radiant energy, F13
Radiation, F13, F34
Radio waves, F26
Radius, bone, A53
Rain, D12, D18, D22–D23, D49
Rain gauge, D23

Rainbow, F16
Rainforests
    destruction of, C61
    ecosystems, B14, B24–B25
    flowers in, A24–A25
    as habitat, B60, B61
Ramps, F100
Rats, A102
Reactants, E67, E69, E70
Reaction to surroundings,
    A7, A90–A94
Recycling materials,
    C62–C63
Recycling matter, B46–B50
Red blood cells, A43, A48
Redwood trees, A66
Reflection, of light, F14
Reflex, A100
Refraction, of light, F14
Reis, Johann, F26
Renewable resources,
    C40–C44
Reproduction
    of animals, A70–A72
    as a life process, A6–A7,
      A72
    of living things, A6–A7,
      A64–A65, A70–A72,
      B26
    of plants, A64–A65, B26
    see also Life cycles
Reptiles, A70
Respiratory system,
    A40–A41, A46–A49
Reusing materials, C62–C63
Revolution, of planets, D72
Rezazadeh, Hossein, A56
Rhinoceros beetle, A56–A57
Ribs, bones, A52, A53
Robotics engineer, F105
Rock cycle, C10, C54
Rocks
    and erosion, C28
    formation of, C6–C7, C54
    layers of, C20–C23
    in soil, C52

    types of, C8–C9
    and weathering, C8, C10,
      C26–C29
Roller coasters, F1, F112
Roller skates, F96–F97
Root systems, A20
Roots, A18–A20, A22, C27
Rotation
    of Earth, D68–D69, D72,
      D78
    of Moon, D71
    of planets, D72
Rusting metal, E27–E28,
    E68

S

Saber-toothed tigers, B79,
    D38
Saliva, A34
Salt water, E58–E60
Sand
    melting, E74–E75
    mixtures of, E54, E58,
      E60
    and soil, C53
    solubility of, E60
Saturn, D57, D59, D65, D72
Scarlet macaws, B24
Scavengers, B46–B48
Screw, F101
Sea anemone, B23
Sea breeze, D24
Sea otters, A93, A102
Sea stacks, C26–C27
Sea slug, B62
Sea stars, A79, A80
Sea turtles, A100
Sea water, E58–E59
Seahorse, B83
Seals, A80, D34
Seasons, D68–D69
Secret World of Spiders,
   The, A75
Sediment, C8, C29

Sedimentary rock, C8–C10
Seed dispersal, B26
Seeds
    from flowers, A19,
      A64–A65, B26
    from fruits, B26
    germinating, A65
    planting, A66
    scattering, B26
    sprouting, A64
Seeing, A90
Seismologist, C65
Sense organs, A90–A93
Series circuit, F57
Severe weather, D28
Shackleton, Sir Ernest,
    D30–D31
Shade, B7
Shadows, F13
Shape, of matter, E6, E24
Shelter, B22, B25
Sierra Club, B72
Sierra Nevada Mountains,
    C30
Silent Spring, B42–B43
Silt, C53
Simmons, Philip, E50
Simple machines,
    F100–F103
Single-celled organisms,
    A10
Skates, F96–F97
Skeletal muscle, A54
Skeletal system, A52–A53
Skin, A90
Skull, A53
Skunks, B25, B38–B39, D34
Skydiving, F94
Sleet, D18
Sloths, A96–A97
Small intestine, A36
Smelling, A90, A93
Smooth muscle, A54
Snakes, A93, B40
Snow, D18, E62–E63
Snowboard, F93

Soil
  destruction of, C61
  erosion of, C28
  in forest ecosystem, B7
  layers of, C52
  makeup of, B6
  minerals in, C52
  as natural resource, C44,
    C52–C53
  nutrients in, B48–B50,
    C44, C52
  pollution of, C60
  properties of, C52–C53
  rocks in, C52
  types of, C53
Soil horizons, C52
Soil mites, C66–C67
Soil profile, C52
Solar cells, F107
**Solar energy systems
  installer,** C65
Solar eruptions, D82–D83
Solar power, C51
Solar system, D50–D51,
    D56–D57, D64–D65, D79
Solids
  changes in, E48–E49
  mass of, E14–E16
  and mixtures, E56
  particles of, E44–E45,
    E48–E49
  properties of, E8–E10
  volume of, E17
Solubility, E60
Solutions, E58–E60
Sound, F20–F24, F36–F37
Sound energy, F8, F20–F21
Sound waves, A92,
    F22–F23
South Pole, D25, D38
Space probes, D65
Species, B70
Speed, and motion, F84–F85
Spiders, A75, A101, B83
Spine, A52

Spirit, Mars rover, D65
Spring scale, E18
Springs, F7, F20
Stamen, A64, A65
Starches, A34
Stars, D1, D76–D79
State, changes in, E48–E49
Static electricity, F44–F46
Steam, E8, E10
Stems, A18–A19, A21, A22
Stimuli, A90–A94
Stomach, A32, A35
Stratosphere, D9
Stratus clouds, D17
Strip mining, C48
Succulents, A20
Sugar
  as carbohydrate, A34
  chemical changes in,
    E70–E71
  and photosynthesis, A22,
    B36
  physical changes of,
    E70–E71
  solubility of, E60
Sun
  diameter of, D48, D51
  and Earth, D48–D49, D56
  energy from, B36, C51,
    D48–D49, D76
  heat from, D7, D10, D24,
    D48–D49, D76, F13
  light from, D76, F13
  mass of, D51
  orbiting, D50–D51,
    D68–D69
  and solar eruptions,
    D82–D83
  and solar system,
    D50–D51, D56–D57,
    D64–D65, D79
  surface of, D51
  and water cycle, D16,
    D49

Tadpole, A80
Tamarin monkey, B25
Tapir, B24
Taproot system, A20
Tasting, A90, A92
Telephone, F26–F27
Telescopes, D64
Temperate climate, D35
Temperate zone, B15, D35
Temperature, D23, D25,
    E46–E49, F30–F31
Termites, A106–A107
Terrarium, B16
Texture, of matter, E6, E25
Thermal energy
  changes in, E44–E50
  heat from, E45, F30–F32
  and matter, E44–E45
  and radiant energy, F13
  and temperature,
    E46–E47, F30–F31
  transfer of, F8, F32–F33
Thermometers, D23,
    E46–E47
Thermosphere, D9
Thorn bug, A52
Throat, A40
Thunderstorms, D26–D27,
    D40–D41
Tibia, bone, A53
Tissues, A12, A32, A54
Titan, moon of Saturn, D65
Titan arum, flower,
    A24–A25
Topsoil, C52
Tornadoes, D26, D28,
    D40–D41
Toucan, B60
Touching, A90
Trachea, A40, A41
Traits, A79–A80
Trash, C60–C63, E30–E31

Trees
life cycle of, A64
life span of, A66
as producers, B24
as renewable resources, C41
rings of, D38
as shelter, B25
see also Plants
Trillium plants, B12–B13
Trilobites, B79
Triton, moon of Neptune, D62
Tropical air masses, D25
Tropical climate, D35
Tropical fish, D34
Troposphere, D8–D9
Tundra habitat, B61

Ulna, bone, A53
Universe, D76, D79. *See also* Solar system
Uranus, D57, D60, D64, D72
Ursa Major, D78

Vacuoles, A8–A9
Veins, A42–A43
Velociraptor, B79
Velocity, F86
Ventricles, heart, A44
Venus, D56, D57, D72
Vertebra, bones, A53
Vibrations, F20–F21, F23
Villi, A36
Vitamins, A33
Volcanoes, C16–C18, C32–C33
Voles, B38, B40
Volume
sound, F22
spatial, E14–E15, E17

Volvox, A11
Voyager 2, D60

Warm air mass, D26, D37
Warm climates, D34–D35
Warning coloration, B63
Water
and deposition, C29
on Earth, C42, D14
and erosion, C28
in forest ecosystem, B7
as natural resource, C40, C42–C43
for plants, A22
states of, D14–D15, E8
warming of, D24, D34, D36, D48
Water cycle, C42, D16, D49
Water droplets, D17
Water vapor
and clouds, D17
and condensation, C42
and evaporation, C42, D15–D16, D49, E49
as gas, D14, E8–E9
and precipitation, D37
Watson, Thomas, F26
Wavelength, F12, F16, F22
Waves, of energy, F12–F15, F22–F23, F26–F27
Weather,
and atmosphere, D9
data, D22, D27
factors of, D22–D23
forecasts, D27, D28
fronts, D26, D27
maps, D27
patterns of, D26
Weathering, C8, C10, C26–C29
Wedge, F101
Weight, D52, E18
Whales, A101–A102, B64, F36–F37

Wheel and axle, F102
Wheels, F93, F96–F97
White blood cells, A43
Wildfires, C18
Wind
causes of, D24, D48
and deposition, C29
and erosion, C28
measuring, D23
and weather, D22
Windpipe, A41
Wind power, C51
Wind speed, D23, D41
Wood duck, B60
Woodchucks, B25
Woodpecker, B40
Woolly mammoths, B78, D38

Yellowstone National Park, B72

Zebras, B64

Credits

Permission Acknowledgments

Excerpt from *The Secret World of Spiders*, by Theresa Greenaway, illustrated by Tim Hayward and Stuart Lafford. Copyright © 2001 Steck-Vaughn Company. Reprinted by permission of Steck-Vaughn Company, an imprint of Harcourt Education International. Excerpt from "Arachne the Spider" from the *Orchard Book of Greek Myths*, retold by Geraldine McCaughrean, illustrated by Emma Chichester Clark. First published in the U.K. by Orchard Books in 1992. Text copyright © 1992 by Geraldine McCaughrean. Illustrations copyright © 1992 by Emma Chichester Clark. Reprinted by permission of The Watts Publishing Group and Margaret K. McElderry Books, an imprint of Simon & Schuster Children's Publishing Division. Excerpt from "The Alligator" from *The Florida Water Story: From Raindrops to the Sea*, by Peggy Sias Lantz and Wendy A. Hale. Copyright © 1998 by Peggy Sias Lantz and Wendy A. Hale. Reprinted by permission of Pineapple Press, Inc. Excerpt from *Animals in Danger: Florida Manatee*, by Rod Theodorou. Copyright © 2001 by Reed Educational & Professional Publishing. Reprinted by permission of Harcourt Education. Excerpt from "The Search" from *The Midnight Fox*, by Betsy Byars, illustrated by Ann Grifalconi. Copyright © 1968 by Betsy Byars. Reprinted by permission of Viking Penguin, A Division of Penguin Young Readers Group, A Member of Penguin Group (USA) Inc., 345 Hudson Street, New York, NY 10014. All rights reserved. Excerpt from *Crafty Canines: Coyotes, Foxes, and Wolves*, by Phyllis J. Perry. Copyright © 1999 by Franklin Watts. All rights reserved. Reprinted by permission of Franklin Watts, an imprint of Scholastic Library Publishing. Excerpt from "First Snow: A Native American Myth" from *The Golden Hoard: Myths and Legends of the World* by Geraldine McCaughrean, illustrated by Bee Willey. Text copyright © 1995 by Geraldine McCaughrean. Illustrations copyright © 1995 by Bee Willey. Reprinted by permission of Orion Children's Books and Margaret K. McElderry Books, an imprint of Simon & Schuster Children's Publishing Division.

Cover

(Lizard) JH Pete Carmichael/Getty Images. (Rock) Digital Vision/Getty Images. (Desert bkgd) Photodisc/Getty Images. (Back cover lizard) (Spine) © David A Northcott/CORBIS. (Cactus) © George H. H. Huey/CORBIS.

Photography

Unit A Opener: Anup Shah/Nature Picture Library. **A1** Merlin D. Tuttle/Bat Conservation International. **A2–A3** (bkgd) Darrell Gulin/DRK photo. **A3** (b) David Noton Photography/Alamy Images. (tr) Claudia Kunin/Corbis. **A4** (bl) Mattias Klum/ National Geographic/Getty Images. **A4–A5** (bkgd) Freeman Patterson/Masterfile. **A6** (b) J. David Andrews/Masterfile. (bl) GK Hart/ Vikki Hart/Photodisc/Getty Images. **A7** (tl) John Beedle/Alamy Images. (tr) David Young–Wolff/Photo Edit Inc. (cl) M. T. Frazie/ Photo Researchers, Inc. (cr) Francois Gohier/ Photo Researchers, Inc. **A7** (bl) © Dwight Kuhn Photography. (br) Gail M. Shumway/ Bruce Coleman Inc **A8** © Dwight Kuhn Photography. **A9** Carolina Biological/Visuals Unlimited/Getty Images. **A10** (l) © E.R. Degginger/Dembinsky Photo Associates. (r) S. Lowry/Univ Ulster/Stone/Getty Images. **A11** (r) © Bill Curtsinger/National Geographic/Getty Images. (l) Kim Taylor/Bruce Coleman Inc. **A12** (tl) Peter Weber/ Photograper's Choice/Getty Images. (c) William b. Rhoten. **A13** (t) GK Hart/Vikki Hart/Photodisc/Getty Images. (c) Kim Taylor/ Bruce Coleman Inc. (b) Peter Weber/ Photograper's Choice/Getty Images. **A14** (br) The Granger Collection. (tl) The Granger Collection. (Frame) Image Farm. **A15** (cr) Omikron/Photo Researchers, Inc. (b) © 1998 from the Warnock Library. Imaged by Octavo (www.octavo.com). Used with permission. **A16** (bl) Art Wolfe/The Image Bank/Getty Images. **A16–A17** (bkgd) Stephen J. Krasemann/DRK photo. **A18** Gary Braasch/Corbis. **A19** Peter Chadwick/DK Images. **A20** (tl) © E.R. Degginger/Photo Researchers, Inc. (cl) A. Pasieka/Photo Researchers, Inc. (bl) Richard Parker/Photo Researchers, Inc. (bc) Michael Boys/Corbis. (br) Michael P. Gadomski/Photo Researchers, Inc. **A21** (bl) Photri. (t) R. A. Mittermeier/ Bruce Coleman Inc. (br) Steve Gorton/DK Images. **A23** (t) Peter Chadwick/DK Images. (c) Michael Boys/Corbis. **A28–A29** (bkgd) Philippe Montigny/Vandystandt/The Image Pro Shop Ltd. **A29** (tr) Pete A. Eising/ Stockfood Munich/Stockfood America. (c) Roy Morsch/Corbis. (br) Lester Lefkowitz/ Corbis. **A30** (bl) John Burwell/Foodpix. **A30–A31** (bkgd) Gladden Willis, M. d./Visuals Unlimited. **A35** (tl) © E.R. Degginger/Color Pic, Inc. **A38–A39** Stephen Frink/Corbis. **A40** (bl) Charles V. Angelo/Photo Researchers, Inc. **A41** Pemberton/Photri Inc. **A43** (tr) P. Motta & S. Correr/Photo Researchers, Inc. **A50** (bl) Lawrence Migdale. **A50–A51** (bkgd) P. Leonard/Zefa/Masterfile. **A52** (bl)Frank Greenaway/DK Images. (r) Dave Roberts/ Science Photo Library. **A54** Steve Shott/DK Images. **A55** (b) Steve Shott/DK Images. **A60–A61** (bkgd) Michel & Christine Denis– Hout/Photo Researchers, Inc. **A61** (tr) Keith Brofsky/Getty Images. (c) Jane Sapinsky/ Superstock. (br) John Daniels/Ardea London Ltd. (bl) Dennis Flaherty/Photo Researchers, Inc. **A62–A63** (bkgd) Marc Moritsch/National Geographic Image Collection. **A68** (bl) Tom Lazar/Earth Scenes/Animals Animals. **A68–A69** (bkgd) Steve Maslowski/Visuals Unlimited. **A70** (tc) Marty Cordano/DRK photo. (tr) Joe McDonald/Bruce Coleman Inc. (b) Jerry Young/DK Images **A71** (l) Alan & Linda Detrick/Photo Researchers, Inc. (t) Gilbert S. Grant/Photo Researchers, Inc. (b) Kent Wood/Photo Researchers, Inc. (r) Bill Beatty. **A73** (t) Marty Cordano/DRK Photo. (c) Gilbert S. Grant/Photo Researchers, Inc. **A75** (bkgd) Kim Taylor/Bruce Coleman Inc. **A76** (b) Bahr/Picturequest. **A76–A77** (bkgd) Charles Krebs/Corbis. **A78** T Davis/ W Bilenduke/Getty Images. **A79** (c) W. Schroll/ Zefa/Masterfile. (t) Frans Lanting/Minden Pictures. (b) Sylvaine Achernar/The Image bank/Getty Images. **A80** (b) Dan Guravich/ Corbis. (c) Dan Suzio/Photo Researchers, Inc. (t) Breck P. Kent/ Earth Scenes/Animals Animals. **A86–A87** (bkgd) David A Northcott/Corbis. **A87** (b) Sanford/ Agliolo/ Corbis. (c) John Eastcott & Yva Momatiuk/ Natinal Geographic Image Collection. **A88** (bl) John Daniels/Ardea. **A88–A89** (bkgd) T. Ozonas/Masterfile. **A90** (bl) Michael D. L. Jordan/Dembinsky Photo Associates, Inc. **A90** (br) © E.R. Degginger/Color Pic, Inc. **A91** (tl) David Sieren/Visuals Unlimited. (tr) David Sieren/Visuals Unlimited. (br) Michael Quinton/Minden Pictures. **A92** (b) Stephen Dalton/NHPA. (t) Frank Greenaway/DK Images. **A93** (t) J. Westrich/Zefa/Masterfile. (b) Stephen J. Krasemann/DRK Photo. **A94** (b) © Dwight Kuhn Photography. (t) Adam Jones/Visuals Unlimited. **A95** (t) Michael Quinton/Minden Pictures. (c) J. Westrich/ Zefa/Masterfile. (b) © Dwight Kuhn Photography. **A96** (br) Geoff Dann/DK Images. **A96–A97** (bkgd) Gergory Dimijian/ Science Photo Library/Photo Researchers, Inc. **A97** (tr) Urs Hauenstein/Photo Atlas. **A98** (bl) Steve Bloom/Alamy Images. **A98–A99** (bkgd) Adam Jones/Photo Researchers, Inc. **A100–101** (bkgd) Mike Parry/Minden Pictures. **A101** (br) Mitsuaki Iwago/Minden Pictures. (tr) Stephen J. Krasemann/DRK Photo. **A102** Jack Sullivan/ Alamy Images. **A103** (cr) Lawrence Migdale. (b) Herbert Kehrer/Photo Researchers, Inc. **A105** (tl) Jackson Smith/Alamy Images. (br) LWA-Dan Tardif/Corbis. (bkgd) Phototone Abstracts. Unit B Opener: Doug Perrine/Sea Pics. **B1** Jeff Jaskolski/Sea Pics. **B2–B3** (bkgd) J. Schultz /T. Soucek/AlaskaStock.com. **B3** (tr) George Ranalli/Photo Researchers, Inc. (c) Georgette Douwma/Photographer's Choice/ Getty Images. (br) Karl Maslowski/Photo Researchers, Inc. **B4–B5** (bkgd) Terry W. Eggers/Corbis. **B7** John Anderson/Animals Animals. **B8** (t) RGK Photography/Stone/Getty Images. (b) Jeff Foott/Bruce Coleman, Inc. **B9** (t) John Anderson/Animals Animals. (c) Jeff Foott/ Bruce Coleman, Inc. (b) RGK Photography/ Stone/Getty Images. **B10** (bl) Lynda Richardson/Corbis. **B10–B11** (bkgd) Michael Fogden/DRK Photo. **B12** (bl) John Anderson/ Animals Animals. **B14** (t) Art Wolfe. (b) Jake Rajs/Stone/Getty Images. **B15** (b) Ralph Krubner/Index Stock Imagery, Inc. (t) Steve Dunwell/Index Stock Imagery, Inc. **B17** (c) Ralph Krubner/Index Stock Imagery, Inc. **B19** (tr) Tom and Pat Leeson/Photo Researchers, Inc. (bkgd) Galen Rowell/Corbis. **B20** (bl) Michael Fogden/DRK Photo. **B20–B21** (bkgd) © Dwight Kuhn Photography. **B22** P. Sharpe/ OSF/Animals Animals. **B23** (cl) Norbert Wu/ DRK Photo. (b) Warren Photographic. **B26** (bl) © E.R. Degginger/Color Pic, Inc. (br) Gregory K. Scott/Photo Researchers, Inc. **B27** (t) P. Sharpe/OSF/Animals Animals. (b) © E.R. Degginger/Color-Pic, Inc. **B32–B33** (bkgd) Ahup Shah/DRK Photo. **B33** (tc) George D. Lepp/Photo Researchers, Inc. (cr) R. Ian Lloyd/Masterfile. **B34–B35** J. Borris/Zefa/ Masterfile. **B38** (l) © E.R. Degginger/Color Pic, Inc. (r) Paul Sterry/Worldwide Picture Library/Alamy Images. **B39** (l) Konrad Wothe/Minden Pictures. (r) Jeremy Woodhouse/Pixelchrome.com. **B41** (c) Paul Sterry/Worldwide Picture Library/Alamy Images. **B42** (c) Esselte Corporation. **B42–43** (bkgd) Jason Stone/Leeson Photography. **B43** (tl) Bettmann/Corbis. (frame) Image Farm. **B44–B45** Mike Lane/Photo Researchers, Inc. **B46** Jack Wilburn/Animals Animals. **B47** (b) Nigel J Dennis/NHPA. (tr) Kenneth W. Fink/Photo Researchers, Inc. **B49** Donald Specker/Animals Animals. **B50** Wally Eberhart/Visuals Unlimited. **B51** (t) Mike Lane/Photo Researchers, Inc. **B56–B57** (bkgd) © Norbert Wu. **B57** (tr) David Cavagnaro/Peter Arnold, Inc. (br) Ken Lucas/ Visuals Unlimited. (c) Lloyd Cluff/Corbis. **B58** (bl) Anne DuPont. **B58–B59** (bkgd) Brandon D. Cole/Corbis. **B60** Sharon Cummings/ Dembinsky Photo Associates. **B61** (bl) C.K. Lorenz/Photo Researchers, Inc. (br) John Eastcott/YVA Momatiuk/Photo Researchers, Inc. (tr) Michael Fogden/DRK Photo. (tl) Nigel J. Dennis; Gallo Images/Corbis. **B62** (cr) Wayne Lankinen/DRK Photo. (bl) © E.R. Degginger/Color-Pic, Inc. **B63** (c) Buddy

Assignment

Illustration

Extreme Science

Nature of Science

Health and Fitness Handbook